Mathematical Origami

Making robust polyhedra from simple units folded from photocopy paper

David Mitchell

Tarquin

About the author

David Mitchell was for many years a professional contract author and paperfolding designer. He is now retired but does not notice that much has changed. He seems to work as hard as ever, though usually nowadays without pay.

Details of his designs, and in many cases folding diagrams showing how to make them, can be found on his website www.origamiheaven.com

There is a section of the site specifically devoted to mathematical paperfolding at www.origamiheaven.com/education.htm

© David Mitchell 2020
ISBN Paperback: 978-1-91109-303-9
ISBN Cased: 978-1-91109-316-9
ISBN EBook: 978-1-91109-348-0
Designed by Versatile PreMedia
Printed in Europe
Distributed in the USA by IPG: www.ipgbook.com

Tarquin
Suite 74, 17 Holywell Hill
St Albans AL1 1DT
UK
www.tarquingroup.com

Contents

Introduction

This book shows you how to make a range of robust polyhedra from ordinary photocopy paper using a technique known as modular origami. Modular origami designs are made by first folding several, or sometimes many, sheets of paper into simple individual modules and then by putting these modules together, normally without the help of any kind of adhesive, to create a finished polyhedral form.

These finished polyhedra can be used in the classroom in the same way as polyhedra made using other techniques. However there are several distinct advantages to making polyhedra using modular origami:

- The process of creating the necessary starting shapes and of folding the modules is itself highly mathematical in nature.
- Modules / polyhedra can be made as group projects.
- A complete set of modules for a polyhedron can be used as an assembly puzzle.
- Finished polyhedra can be taken apart and the modules re-used to build other polyhedra of the same class.
- Modules can be swapped around within the same polyhedral form to create different surface colourings.
- The modules can be taken apart and stored flat until the next time they are required.
- Damaged modules can easily be replaced.

When the first edition of this book was published in 1999 modular origami was still a relatively new form of paperfolding. Modular origami design has moved on since then and I am delighted to have the opportunity to expand and revise this book to present both a wider range of designs, and to introduce new designs which are more robust and offer more potential for mathematical adventures.

In order to keep the folding sequences as simple as possible the designs are made from five different starting shapes, the square, the 1:√2 or silver rectangle, the 1:√3 or bronze rectangle, the golden rectangle and a rectangle, which for want of a better term, I call the mock platinum rectangle. This last rectangle easily yields angles which approximate pentagonal angles sufficiently closely for the purposes of a classroom model. Using a range of starting shapes, rather than, for instance, just squares, offers the additional advantage that related modules of differing geometries can easily be created by applying the same sequence of folds to the various rectangles in turn. Instructions for simple ways to create each of the starting rectangles are given at the end of the book.

How to follow the folding instructions

Paperfolding instructions are a sequence of pictures that show each individual step you need to take to progress from the starting shape to the finished design. Most of the pictures (except the first and last) are both 'before' and 'after' diagrams. They show you the result of making the previous fold and give you instructions for making the next one.

Typical diagrams for a simple folding sequence might look like this.

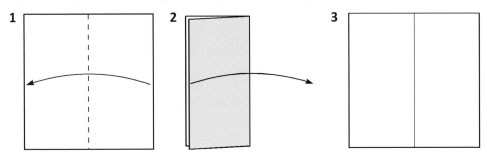

In picture 1, the fold arrow tells you to fold the paper in half from right to left by laying the right edge onto the left edge and flattening the paper to form a crease in the position marked by the dashed fold line.

Picture 2 shows the result of making the fold. You will see that although the two layers at the left edge should now lie exactly on top of each other, this picture shows them slightly offset. This is so that you can see how many layers of paper are in each place. The fold arrow without a fold line in this picture gives you the next instruction and tells you to undo the fold you have just made.

Picture 3 shows the result of following the first two instructions. You have made a vertical crease down the centre of the paper. This crease is marked with a thin line.

This sequence of diagrams could be compressed into just one picture, which would look like this:

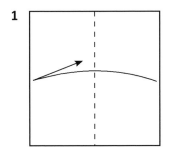

In this case the fold arrow and fold line combination tell you to make the fold, crease it firmly, then unfold it again.

In some of the diagrams you will come across another type of fold line, one that is made up of dots as well as dashes. This is used to show that a fold has to be made in the opposite direction to the normal, dashes-only, fold line. Here's an example of how it works:

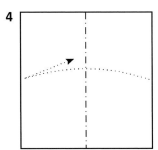

You can look at this picture as the fourth instruction in the sequence we began with. You have already made a vertical crease in the centre of the paper and this instruction now tells you to fold the left hand half of the paper backwards behind the right hand half using the crease as a hinge. The dotted and dashed fold line tells you the fold is made backwards and the dotted fold arrow tells you that the fold is made behind the paper rather than in front of it. Dotted lines can also be used to show you other details like edges which are hidden underneath the front layers of the paper.

There are also a few other symbols that you need to understand the meaning of:

 The turnover arrow tells you to turn the paper over sideways before making the next fold. If you find your paper no longer looks like the diagrams you may well have missed seeing one of these.

 This kind of arrow tells you that the next picture has been drawn to a larger scale.

 This kind of arrow tells you to apply pressure to some point. It is usually used when a corner needs to be turned inside out or when modules need to be pressed together.

 This kind of arrow tells you to pull out some part of the paper in the direction of the arrow.

 Assembly arrows show you where a tab has to be inserted into a pocket during the assembly phase of the design. If the arrow is behind the front layer of paper it will be shown in grey instead of black.

Tips on folding

- It is easiest to fold with your paper laid on a flat, smooth surface. If you want to relax in the arm-chair while you fold then use a coffee-table type hardback on your lap. Folding in the air is strictly for experts or for the birds.

- Don't be afraid to turn your paper around so that you can make the fold in the most natural way. The diagrams have been drawn to explain the folds not to tell you how to make them. What would be perfectly comfortable for a right-handed person might be torture to a left-handed one. Always remember to re-align your paper to the diagrams when you have finished making the fold though.

- The best tools for sharpening up creases are strong fingernails, but if you have none, or if, like mine, they are worn out through too much folding, then the curved parts of knife or scissor handles, or anything similarly tough and rounded, can be used instead.

- Each time you finish a fold check that none of the edges or corners have been pulled out of true. If they have, correct them.

- Treat the paper gently. Handling it roughly will cause crumpling which will spoil the clean look of the finished design.
- If despite this your paper goes floppy through too much handling you can restore it by opening it fully out and ironing it with a slightly warm dry iron. The creases will be easy to re-fold since the lines of weakness will still be there. This is a good way of smartening up old models, but beware - too much heat will cause the edges of the paper to curl.

Tips on putting the modules together

- Fold all the modules before you start putting them together.
- Be as gentle with the modules during assembly as you were with the paper while you were folding it. There is an element of puzzle involved in constructing any modular assembly. Enjoy it!
- The last module is always the most difficult to ease into place. If it's a case of getting a reluctant flap into a pocket then curling the flap slightly often helps. Otherwise try loosening the surrounding modules a bit.

If all the modules are in place but you can't get them to fit tightly together try just easing each module a tiny bit inwards at a time. Alternatively it may be that all the modules that meet at one point need to be pushed together in one go. Every design is different. There just aren't any rules.

Tips on using glue

Nearly all the designs in this book will hold firmly together by themselves, but there are degrees of stability. Some are so completely robust they could safely be tossed across the room. Others require more delicate handling. There is nothing wrong in gluing the less stable designs together but don't overdo it. If you make a fold in the wrong place you can always unfold it and try again, but once you have glued a module in place it is difficult to remove it again without destroying the whole assembly.

And, of course, a design that is glued together cannot be taken apart and stored flat, nor can the modules be re-used as part of another design.

The Cube

The Cube

This wonderful cube was first discovered by the British paperfolder Paul Jackson in the early 1970s and so is often known as the Paul Jackson Cube. It is made from six very simple modules each of which contributes one face to the design.

Somewhat unusually, the modules are not provided with pockets, although they do have tabs, which go inside the design. Because the gaps between the tabs along the open edges of the modules are slightly less wide than the tabs themselves, assembling the modules creates a mutual inwards pressure which acts to keep them locked together. As a result the finished cube is a surprisingly strong construction and can easily withstand being thrown around.

This cube can also function as a puzzle since it is not obvious at first sight how the modules go together, even when shown a finished version.

You will need six squares. Pages 128 and 129 show you how to make squares from A4 or US letter sized paper.

These diagrams show you how to make a cube using two modules in each of three colours arranged so that opposite faces are the same colour. Other arrangements and colourings are possible.

Folding the modules

1
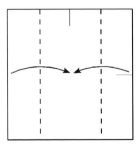

Make a tiny crease to mark the middle of the top edge.

2
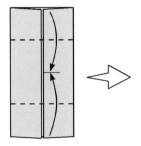

Mark the middle of the right hand edge in a similar way.

3
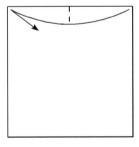

Fold both outside edges to the centre using the crease you made in step 1 as a guide.

4
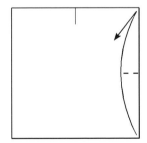

Fold the top and bottom edges to the centre using the crease you made in step 2 as a guide.

5

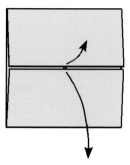

Open up both tabs at right angles.

6

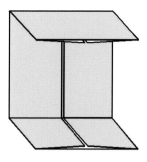

The module is finished. Make six.

Alternatively...

7

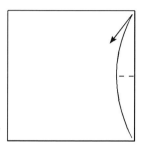

Make a tiny crease to mark the middle of the right hand edge.

8

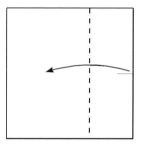

Fold the right edge in a random amount, making sure the top and bottom edges line up.

9

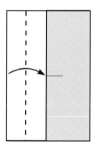

Fold the right edge onto the original left edge.

10

Continue with steps 4 and 5 to produce the finished module.

Putting the modules together

11

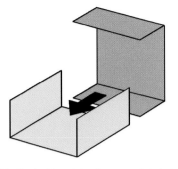

Slide the bottom tab of one module into the open edge of another.

12

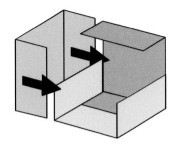

Add the third module to complete one corner...

13

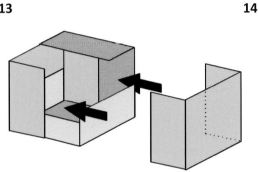

...then add the fourth module like this.

14

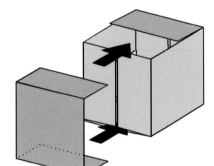

The fifth module slides into place like this.

15

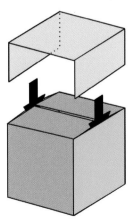

Finally add the sixth module to complete the cube.

16

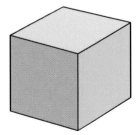

Check that none of the tabs are visible then gently ease all the modules tightly together. If you have made your folds accurately they will lock firmly in place. The cube is finished.

Equilateral Deltahedra

The Regular Tetrahedron

The regular tetrahedron is one of a class of convex polyhedra whose faces are equilateral triangles. In their classic book *Mathematical Models* Cundy and Rollett (see inside back cover) suggest calling these forms convex deltahedra. I believe the term deltahedra is better used to refer to all polyhedra whose faces are all triangles and I prefer to use the more precise term equilateral deltahedra for those whose faces are equilateral triangles. Of the eight possible convex forms in this class, methods for constructing seven can be found in this book.

The regular tetrahedron can be made from just two modules, each of which contributes two faces to the form. Each module is folded from half a 1:√3 or bronze rectangle. Pages 130 and 131 show you how to easily obtain bronze rectangles from A4 or US letter sized paper.

The basic module has four corners each of which can be turned inside out to form a pocket or left as it is to act as a tab. Ten variations of the basic module are therefore possible, each of which can be combined with another module of a different design to form a regular tetrahedron. All of these regular tetrahedra are easy to make and all are equally robust.

Folding the modules

1

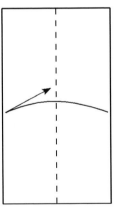

Fold in half sideways, then unfold. When you have done this cut along the vertical crease to separate the two halves of the paper.

2

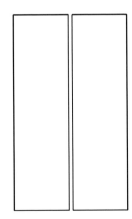

Either half of the paper can be used to fold a module.

3

Fold in half sideways, then unfold.

4

Fold in half downwards, then unfold.

5

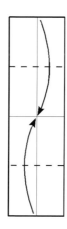

Fold both the top and bottom edges to the centre. The next picture is on a larger scale.

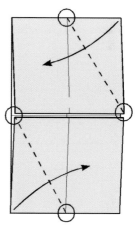

6

Fold the top right and bottom left corners inwards as shown, making sure that the creases begin and end at the points marked with circles. Accuracy is important here.

7

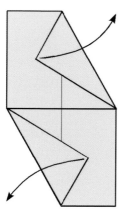

Unfold.

8

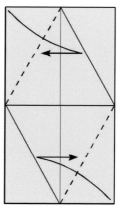

Repeat steps 6 and 7 on the other two corners.

9

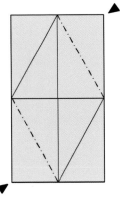

Turn the top right and bottom left corners inside out in between the other layers using the existing creases.

10

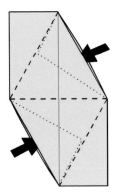

The pockets are marked with arrows. Configure the module to look like picture 12 by folding forwards along the three creases marked with dashed lines here.

11

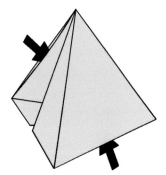

The first module is finished.

Putting the modules together

12

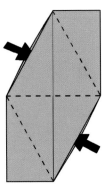

Fold a second module to step 9 but this time create pockets out of the top left and bottom right corners to create a mirror-image module. Configure to look like picture 13.

13

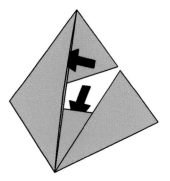

The second module is finished.

14

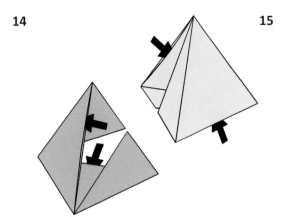
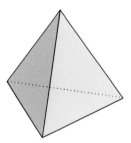

Insert the tabs of one module into the pockets of the other.

15

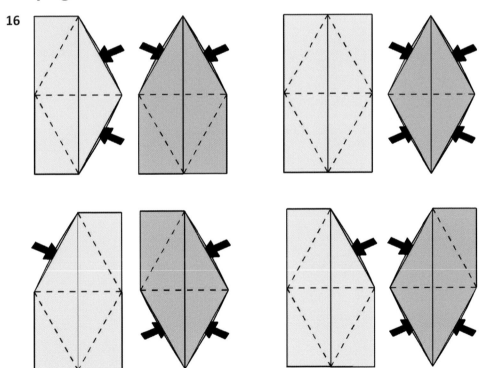

The finished regular tetrahedron should look like this.

Varying the modules

16

There are eight other ways to create a module by turning various numbers of corners inside out to create pockets. Each of the pairs of modules shown here will also go together to form a robust regular tetrahedron.

The Regular Octahedron

Like the regular tetrahedron, the regular octahedron is a convex equilateral deltahedron. It can be made from four modules, each of which contributes two full faces to the form. The same module, which I call the equilateral module, can be used to make several other convex equilateral deltahedra.

Equilateral modules are folded from bronze rectangles. Pages 130 and 131 show you how to easily obtain such rectangles from A4 or US letter sized paper. You will need four bronze rectangles for each regular octahedron. Assembly of the regular octahedron is easier if the tabs of the basic equilateral module are truncated in the way shown on pages 21 and 22.

Despite the fact that they are made from different designs of module, the faces of the regular octahedron and the regular tetrahedron will be the same size provided you begin from the same size of bronze rectangle in each case.

These diagrams show you how to make a regular octahedron in two ways, first by using four identical equilateral modules and then by using two sets of two mirror-image modules. The arrangement of the tabs and pockets of the equilateral module can be varied in other ways to allow other methods of assembling a regular octahedron from a set of four modules of mixed designs.

Folding the modules

1

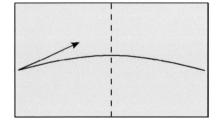

Fold in half sideways, then unfold.

2

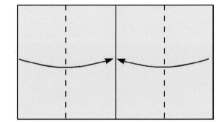

Fold both outside edges onto the vertical centre crease. The next picture is on a larger scale.

3

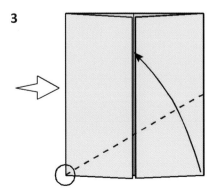

Fold the bottom right corner onto the line where the two outside edges meet in the centre making sure that the new crease begins from the bottom left corner which should become a sharp point.

4

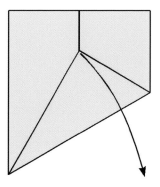

Unfold.

5

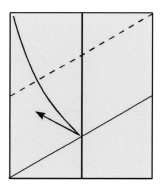

Repeat folds 3 and 4 on the top left corner.

6

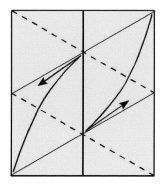

Repeat folds 3 and 4 on the other two corners as well.

7

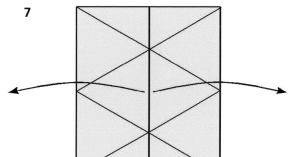

Open out completely.

8

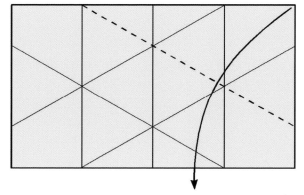

Fold the top right corner diagonally downwards using the existing crease.

9

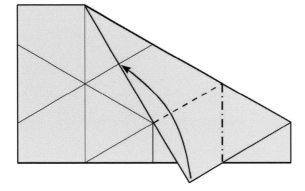

Fold the bottom corner of the front layer diagonally upwards using the existing crease. As you do this the paper will flatten into the form shown in picture 10. Be careful not to make any new creases during this move.

10

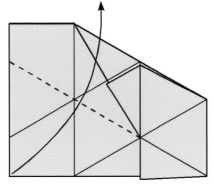

Fold the bottom left corner diagonally inwards underneath the front layers using the existing crease.

11

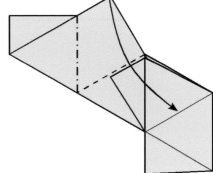

Repeat step 9 on the top corner.

12

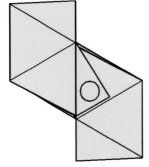

Tuck the flap marked with a circle out of sight underneath the layer behind it.

13

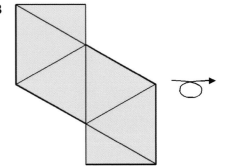

Turn over sideways.

14

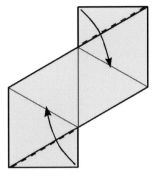

Fold the top and bottom flaps out of sight inside the layers using the existing creases.

15

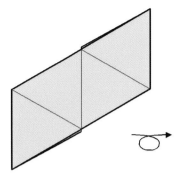

Turn over sideways.

16

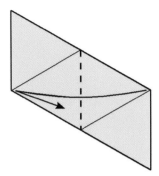

Fold in half sideways, then unfold.

17

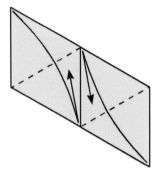

Fold both the top and bottom corners inwards using the existing creases, then unfold.

18

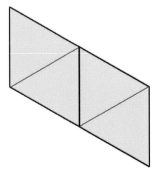

This is the basic module. You can use this basic module to make a regular octahedron but it is easier to assemble if you truncate the ends of the tabs first.

19

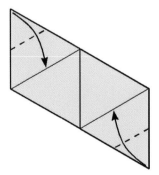

Fold the top and bottom points inwards to the approximate centre of the opposite crease as shown. You should be able to do this sufficiently accurately by eye alone.

20

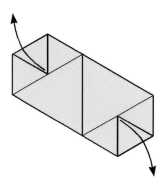

Unfold.

21

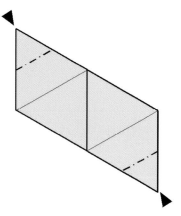

Turn both points inside out in between the other layers using the creases you have just made.

22

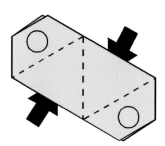

The module has two tabs (marked with circles) and two pockets (marked with arrows). Configure the module by folding it towards you along the creases marked with dashed lines.

23

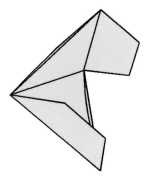

The module is finished. Make all four.

Putting the modules together

24

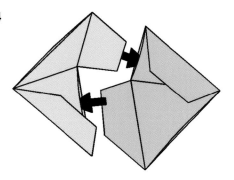

Two modules go together like this to form the back half of the octahedron.

25

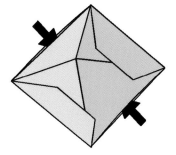

Make another identical assembly and add it to the front making sure that all the tabs slide fully into their pockets.

26

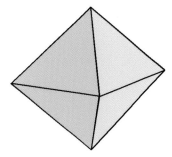

The finished regular octahedron should look like this.

Folding mirror-image modules

You can also make a regular octahedron from two sets of mirror-image modules. Make two modules the original way, fold your other two bronze rectangles to step 8 then follow the instructions here.

27

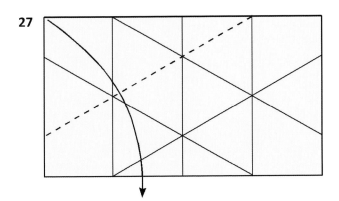

Fold the top left corner diagonally downwards using the existing crease.

28

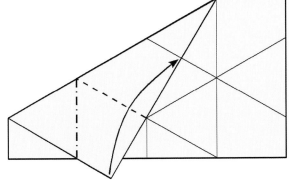

Fold the bottom corner of the front layer diagonally upwards using the existing crease. As you do this the paper will flatten into the form shown in picture 29. Be careful not to make any new creases during this move.

29

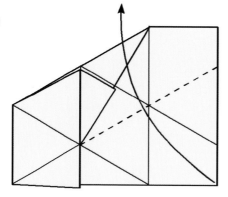

Fold the bottom right corner diagonally inwards underneath the front layers using the existing crease.

30

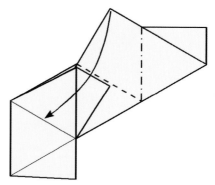

Fold the top corner diagonally downwards using the existing crease. As you do this the paper will flatten into the form shown in picture 31. Be careful not to make any new creases during this move.

31

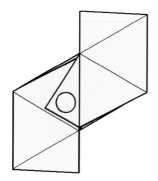

Follow steps 12 through 21 in mirror-image to complete the module and truncate both tabs. The result should look like picture 32.

32

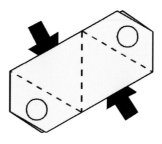

Configure the module by folding it towards you along the creases marked with dashed lines.

Putting the modules together

33

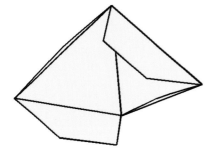

The mirror-image module is finished. Make two.

34

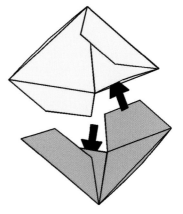

The two mirror-image modules go together like this.

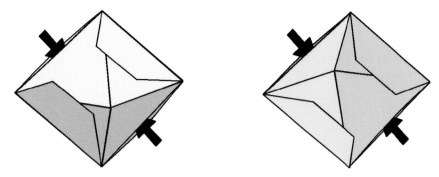

Turn the assembly over and add the mirror-image assembly to an assembly made from the two other modules. Make sure all the tabs are fully inserted in all the pockets.

36

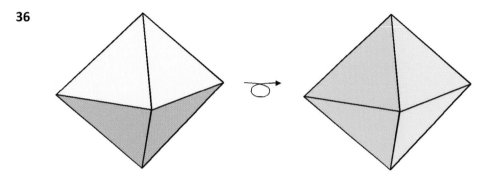

This is what the finished mirror-image module version of the regular octahedron will look like.

Combining regular octahedra and tetrahedra

When made from the same size of starting rectangle (picture 1 on page 14 and picture 1 on page 18) these regular octahedra and tetrahedra have faces of the same size. This allows them to be combined in larger forms.

37

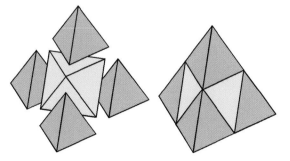

A regular octahedron and four regular tetrahedra can be combined to form a larger compound tetrahedron, like this.

38

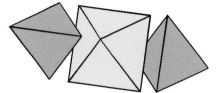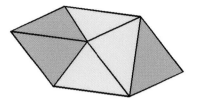

In combination, regular octahedra and regular tetrahedra will fill space. You can see this by placing a regular octahedron and two regular tetrahedra together to make a skew cuboid. Diagrams that show how to make this shape, which I call a diamond hexahedron, from six equilateral modules can be found on pages 29 and 30.

39

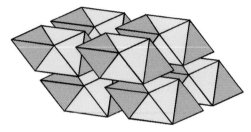

Like all other skew cuboids, the diamond hexahedron will fill space. A simple proof of this is that eight diamond hexahedra will fit together to form a larger diamond hexahedron.

Making other equilateral bi-pyramids

The octahedron can also be seen as an equilateral square bi-pyramid, that is a form made by arranging two square based pyramids with equilateral faces base to base. Equilateral modules will also make the equivalent triangular and pentagonal equilateral bi-pyramids as shown below.

40

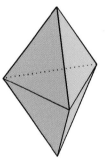

Three equilateral modules will go together to make a triangular equilateral bi-pyramid.

41

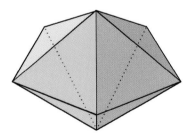

Five equilateral modules will go together to form a pentagonal equilateral bi-pyramid. Because of the wide angle at which the equilateral faces meet this shape is best made from modules whose tabs have not been truncated.

The Regular Icosahedron

The regular icosahedron, which is also a convex equilateral deltahedron, can be made from ten equilateral modules folded as two sets of five mirror-image modules, each of which provides two faces to the design. This design is not as robust as the regular octahedron but it will hold together sufficiently well for most purposes. The assembly process may be a little challenging at first but the result is worth the effort.

Equilateral modules are folded from bronze rectangles. The folding sequence for both the basic modules and the mirror-image modules can be found on pages 18 to 24. It is not necessary to truncate the tabs of the modules.

These diagrams show you how to make a regular icosahedron from two modules in each of five colours. Other colourings are, of course, possible.

Putting the modules together

1

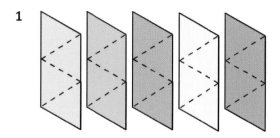

Begin by making ten equilateral modules (see page 18) in two mirror-image sets of five modules each. Arrange the first set of modules to look like this. The surface of the modules that you want to form the outside of the model is at the back. Configure the first set of modules by folding them forwards along the lines marked with dashes then turn them over sideways.

2

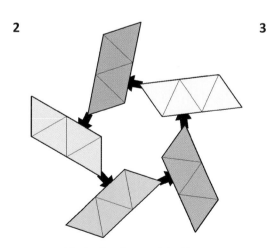

Assemble the first five modules like this to look like picture 3.

3

The first sub-assembly is finished.

4

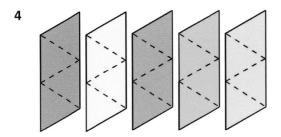

Arrange the second set of modules to look like this. The surface of the modules that you want to form the outside of the model is at the back. Configure the modules by folding them forwards along the lines marked with dashes. Do not turn this set of modules over.

5

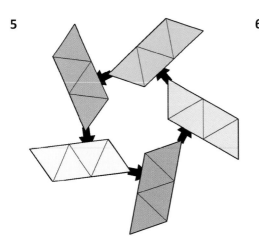

Assemble the second set of modules like this to look like picture 6.

6

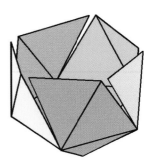

The second sub-assembly is finished.

7

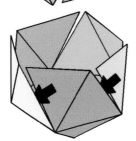

Put the sub-assemblies together by inserting all the flaps of each sub-assembly into the corresponding pockets of the other sub-assembly.

8

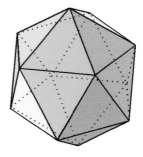

The finished regular icosahedron should look like this.

The Diamond Hexahedron and the Equilateral Hexakaidecahedron

There are two other equilateral deltahedra that can be made from equilateral modules in a very similar way to the regular icosahedron.

Making the diamond hexahedron

A diamond hexahedron has six faces, each of which is a diamond or 60 / 120 degree rhombus. Each of the six modules contributes one face to the design so you will need six modules in all, three in each of two mirror-image sets.

The folding sequence for both the basic modules and the mirror-image modules can be found on pages 18 to 24. It is not necessary to truncate the tabs of the modules.

1   **2**

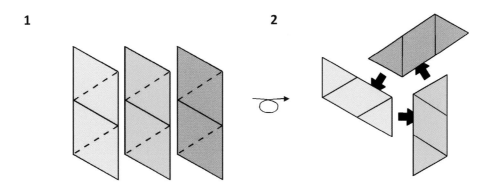

Begin by making six basic equilateral modules in two mirror-image sets of three modules each. Arrange the first set of modules to look like this. The surface of the modules that is to form the outside of the model is at the back. Configure the modules by folding them forwards along the lines marked with dashes then turn them over sideways

Assemble the first set of modules like this to look like picture 3.

3

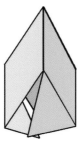

The first sub-assembly is finished.

4

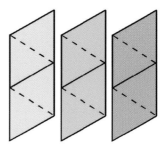

Arrange the second set of modules so that the surface of the modules that is to form the outside of the model is at the back. Configure the modules by folding them forwards along the lines marked with dashes. Do not turn this set of modules over.

5

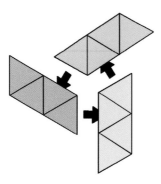

Assemble the second set of modules like this to look like picture 6.

6

The second sub-assembly is finished.

7

Put the sub-assemblies together by inserting all the flaps of each sub-assembly into the corresponding pockets of the other sub-assembly.

8

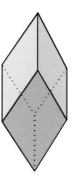

The finished diamond hexahedron should look like this. This hexahedron can also be made by combining two regular tetrahedra with a regular octahedron (see page 26). Diamond hexahedra will fill space.

Making the equilateral hexakaidecahedron

An equilateral hexakaidecahedron has sixteen faces, all of which are equilateral triangles. It is made using two mirror-image sets of four equilateral modules. Each of the eight modules required contributes two faces to the design so you will need eight modules in all, four in each of two mirror-image sets.

The folding sequence for both the basic modules and the mirror-image modules can be found on pages 18 to 24. It is not necessary to truncate the tabs of the modules.

1

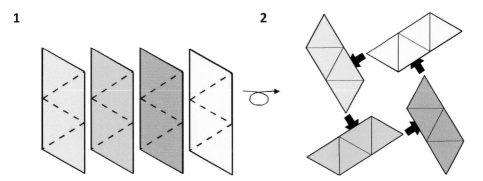

Begin by making eight basic equilateral modules in two mirror-image sets of four modules each. Arrange the first set of modules to look like this. The surface of the modules that is to form the outside of the model is at the back. Configure the first set of modules by folding them forwards along the lines marked with dashes then turn them over sideways.

2

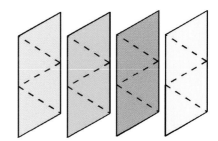

Assemble the first set of modules like this to look like picture 3.

3

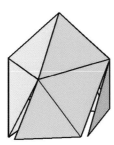

The first sub-assembly is finished.

4

Arrange the second set of modules to look like this. The surface of the modules that is to form the outside of the model is at the back. Configure the modules by folding them forwards along the lines marked with dashes. Do not turn this set of modules over.

5

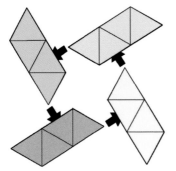

Assemble the second set of modules like this to look like picture 6.

6

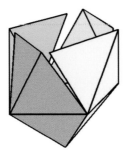

The second sub-assembly is finished.

7

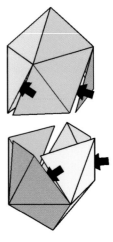

Put the sub-assemblies together by inserting all the flaps of each sub-assembly into the corresponding pockets of the other sub-assembly.

8

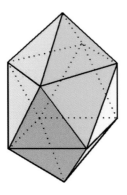

The finished equilateral hexakaidecahedron should look like this. Unlike diamond hexahedra, equilateral hexakeidecahedra will not fill space.

The Equilateral Dodecahedron

The set of convex equilateral deltahedra contains just two more members, the equilateral dodecahedron, which has twelve faces, and the equilateral heccaidecahedron, which has fourteen. Of these, only the dodecahedron can be made using equilateral modules.

Making the equilateral dodecahedron

An equilateral dodecahedron can be made from six equilateral modules arranged in two mirror-image sets of three modules each. Each of the modules contributes two faces to the form.

The folding sequence for both the basic modules and the mirror-image modules can be found on pages 18 to 24. It is not necessary to truncate the tabs of the modules.

1

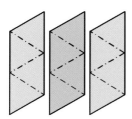

Begin by making six basic equilateral modules in two mirror-image sets of three modules each. Arrange the first set of modules to look like this. The surface of the modules that you want to form the outside of the model is at the front. Configure the first set of modules by folding them backwards along the lines marked with dots and dashes.

2

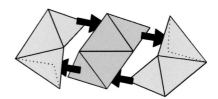

Assemble the first set of modules like this to look like picture 3.

3

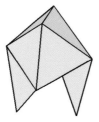

The first sub-assembly is finished.

4

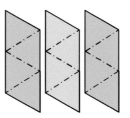

Arrange the second set of modules to look like this. The surface of the modules that you want to form the outside of the model is at the front. Configure the modules by folding them backwards along the lines marked with dots and dashes.

5

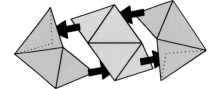

Assemble the second set of modules like this and arrange to look like picture 6.

6

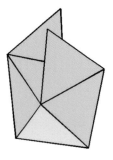

The second sub-assembly is finished.

7

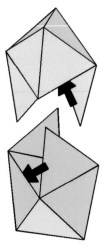

Put the sub-assemblies together by inserting all the flaps of each sub-assembly into the corresponding pockets of the other sub-assembly.

8

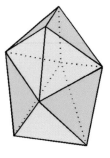

The finished equilateral dodecahedron should look like this. Equilateral dodecahedra will not fill space.

The Regular Dodecahedron

The Regular Dodecahedron

This robust version of the regular dodecahedron is made from thirty modules each of which contributes an edge (and part of two faces) to the form.

It is a common strategy in modular origami to prefer to approximate pentagonal angles rather than attempt to fold them exactly. In this case I have chosen to obtain these approximate angles by using the natural folding geometry of what I call the mock platinum rectangle. This produces angles at the corners of the faces of 108.43 degrees rather than the 108 degrees that would be correct. This difference is within the margin of error of most proficient paperfolders and, in practice, makes little difference to the appearance of the finished design.

Mock platinum rectangles are easily made from squares by following the instructions on pages 132 to 133. You can also make them directly from A4 or US letter sized paper in a similar way.

The folding sequence for the module is the same as the folding sequence for the equilateral module. The module must, however, be configured in a different way at the end of the sequence.

These diagrams show you how to make a regular dodecahedron using six modules in each of five colours. Other colourings are possible.

Folding the modules

Begin by making the thirty mock platinum rectangles required then fold each of them into a basic module by following the folding sequence for the basic equilateral module (steps 1 through 16 on pages 18 to 21).

1

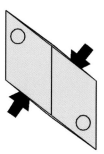

The basic module has two tabs (marked by circles) and two pockets (indicated by arrows). Make six in each of five colours.

2

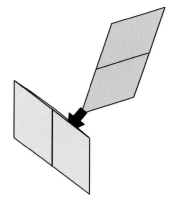

Divide the modules into fifteen pairs. Insert the tab of one module into the pocket of another, like this.

3

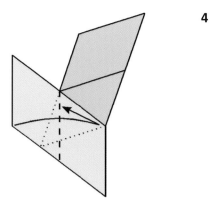

Once the tab is fully inserted into the host module fold the host module in half sideways using the existing crease, then unfold.

4

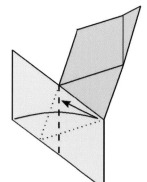

Remove the guest module, turn it round, re-insert it fully and repeat step 4.

5

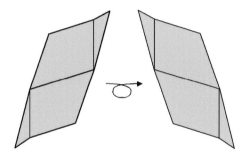

Remove the guest module and turn it over sideways. The first module is finished. Now reverse the roles of the guest and host modules and follow steps 2 through 4 again. Repeat for the other fourteen pairs until all the modules are finished.

Putting the modules together

6

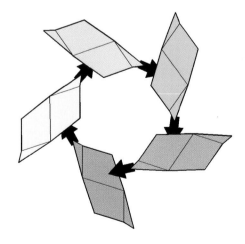

The first five modules go together like this. Note that in each case the tabs of the guest modules slide around the folded edge in the centre of the host module and lock them together. This makes the design very robust but also makes the modules harder to slide into place as assembly progresses.

7

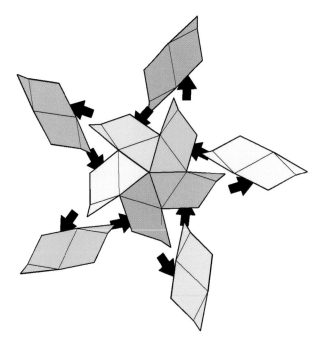

Add five more modules to create the first five vertexes of the dodecahedron. Take care not to damage the tabs of the modules as you ease them into place. Add further modules to complete the form keeping to the colour scheme shown in picture 10.

8

The tabs of the last few modules may prove difficult to slide into place. You can truncate the tabs by folding them in half underneath like this...

9

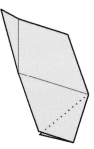

...to make it much easier to finish the assembly without sacrificing too much strength.

10

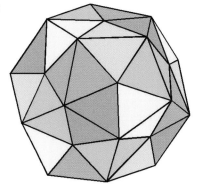

The finished regular dodecahedron should look like this.

Rhombic and Semi-Rhombic Polyhedra

About Silver Rectangles

The designs in this section of the book are, with one exception, folded from 1:√2 or silver rectangles. The term silver rectangle was first adopted as a suitable name for the 1:√2 rectangle by the British Origami Society in 1979 as a result of a suggestion made by the Science section of the Oxford Dictionary, and has since become an established paperfolding term. Mathematicians, however, often refer to the 1:√2 rectangle as the pure rectangle and use the term silver rectangle to refer to the 1:1+√2 rectangle (which is the bit leftover if you cut the largest possible square from a 1:√2 rectangle). In this book the term silver rectangle is used in the paperfolding sense to refer to the 1:√2 rectangle.

The most obviously useful quality of the silver rectangle to a paperfolder is that if you fold it in half short edge to short edge the resulting rectangle is another, half size, silver rectangle. This makes it very easy to scale designs up or down. The process of halving to another silver rectangle in this way can, of course, be continued ad infinitum.

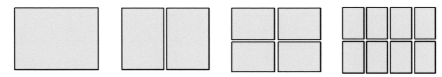

Less obviously, the silver rectangle easily yields the angles necessary for modelling many mathematical forms, such as those explained in this section, and the planar cube and tetrahedron explained elsewhere.

From a modular origami perspective the usefulness of a rectangle is largely determined by the angles that can be obtained by folding corner to corner in both directions, or at which the diagonals cross, which are always the same. The angles obtained by folding the silver rectangle in this way are shown below.

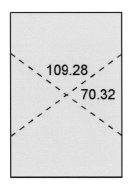
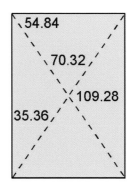

Standard DIN paper sizes, common throughout the world except in the USA, are very close to silver rectangles, the small differences being due to the various sizes being specified in whole millimetres and to cutting variances during manufacture. If you find that you are using DIN paper that is badly out of proportion you can usually diminish the error by folding it short edge to short edge and cutting it in half.

If you do not have easy access to DIN size paper you will need to cut your own silver rectangles from other rectangles such as squares or US letter sized paper. Diagrams showing how how to do this can be found on pages 135 to 137.

If you are not sure whether your paper is a silver rectangle or not you can find out by following the simple procedure below:

1

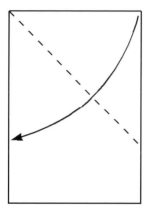

Fold one of the short edges onto one of the long edges.

2

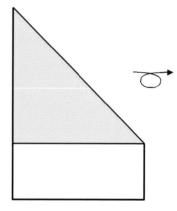

Turn over sideways.

3

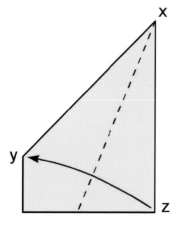

Fold the right hand edge onto the sloping edge so that point x remains sharp.

4

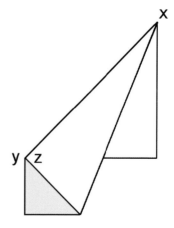

If your paper is a silver rectangle points y and z will lie exactly on top of each other.

About Rhombic and Semi-Rhombic Polyhedra

When I was writing the first edition of this book I found that I wanted to include several polyhedra for which there did not appear to be an established mathematical name. The characteristics of these polyhedra were that their faces were either 109.28/70.32 rhombuses or 70.32/54.84/54.84 triangles, or a mixture of the two, both of which shapes can easily be obtained by folding silver rectangles.

Many such polyhedra have interesting properties, not the least of which is that, as shown on the next few pages, many of them can be combined with copies of themselves to create a rhombic dodecahedron. In addition there are two other interesting solids which can be combined to form a rhombic dodecahedron in this way, and which, while not rhombic polyhedra within my definition, do have some faces that are 70.32/54.84/54.84 (1:√3/2:√3/2) triangles.

For want of anything better, I stole the word 'rhombic' from the name of the rhombic dodecahedron, whose faces are, of course, 109.28/70.32 rhombuses, and applied it to the other polyhedra as well, thus creating the terms rhombic tetrahedron, rhombic octahedron etc and the general term rhombic polyhedra, or solids, to describe them as a group. I justified this usage to myself on the grounds that the triangular faces occurred in pairs, which are derived from a 109.28/70.32 rhombus folded across its shorter diagonal. I was expecting both that I would receive a barrage of criticism for this usage and that someone would soon point out to me a better one, but, somewhat strangely, neither of these things have happened. *Pro tem* then I continue to use the term rhombic polyhedra with this meaning. I use the term 'semi-rhombic' for the other two solids mentioned above.

This nomenclature does raise the difficulty that there are, for instance, several different rhombic polyhedra that could quite properly be called the rhombic hexahedron. To avoid this difficulty I have had to make up other names. One sin inevitably leads to another...

It is also worth pointing out that although the 109.28/70.32 rhombus has diagonals in the proportion 1:√2 I have avoided using the term silver rhombus since that would suggest that this rhombus has properties similar to the silver rectangle, which it does not.

There also is a second set of solids which could equally validly be called rhombic polyhedra whose faces are pairs of 70.32/54.84/54.84 triangles. These can be derived from the 109.28/70.32 rhombus by folding it in half across its longer diagonal. I have not included any of these forms in this book.

1

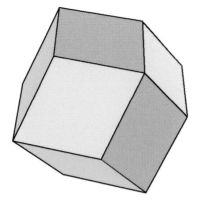

This is a rhombic dodecahedron. It has twelve faces each of which is a 109.29/70.32 degree rhombus.

2

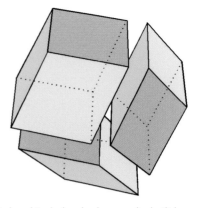

A rhombic dodecahedron can be built by combining four rhombic hexahedra...

3

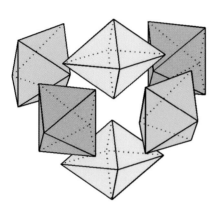

...six rhombic octahedra...

4

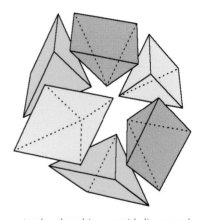

...twelve rhombic pyramids (in several ways)...

5

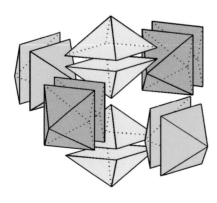

...twelve square-base semi-rhombic pyramids (in several ways)...

6

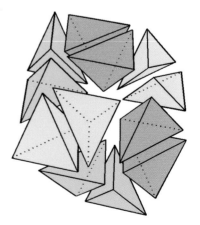

...twenty four rhombic tetrahedra (in several ways)...

7

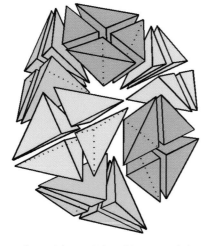

...or forty eight semi-rhombic pyramids (in several ways).

8

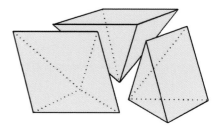

A rhombic hexahedron can be made from three rhombic pyramids...

9

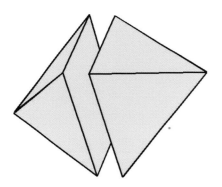

...and a rhombic octahedron from two.

10

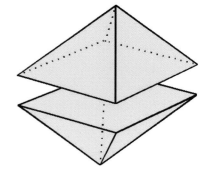

A rhombic octahedron can also be made from two semi-rhombic pyramids...

11

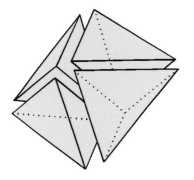

...or four rhombic tetrahedra.

12

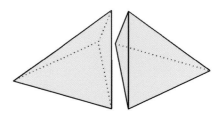

A rhombic pyramid can be made from two rhombic tetrahedra...

13

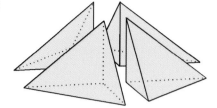

...or four semi-rhombic tetrahedra...

14

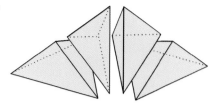

...in several ways.

15

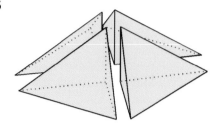

A semi-rhombic pyramid can be made from four semi-rhombic tetrahedra...

16

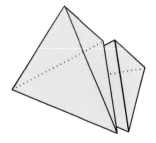

...and a rhombic tetrahedron from two.

17

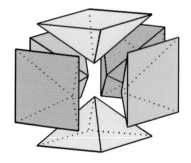

Four semi-rhombic pyramids will also make a cube.

18

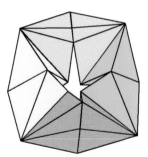

And eight rhombic tetrahedra linked edge to edge in a circle will create a rolling ring.

The Rhombic Dodecahedron

The rhombic dodecahedron has twelve faces each of which is a 109.28/70.32 degree rhombus. This modular origami version is made from twelve rhombic modules, which each contribute one full face to the design. This method was first discovered by the British paperfolder Nick Robinson in 1986.

Each module is folded from a 1:√2 or silver rectangle. A4 paper is a sufficiently close approximation of a silver rectangle to be used for this purpose. Alternatively a method of obtaining silver rectangles from US letter sized paper is given on pages 135 to 137.

A rhombic dodecahedron can be built from, or subdivided into, 4 rhombic hexahedra, 6 rhombic octahedra, 12 rhombic pyramids or square base semi-rhombic pyramids, 24 rhombic tetrahedra or 48 semi-rhombic tetrahedra. Rhombic dodecahedra can also be combined to create other interesting forms.

The volume of a rhombic dodecahedron is twice the volume of a cube inscribed inside it.

Rhombic dodecahedra will fill space.

The position of the tabs and pockets of the rhombic module can be varied. These diagrams show you how to fold the original parallelogram version of the module and a triangular version of my own. It might be an interesting classroom project to fold the modules for both and compare the way they go together.

In both cases the diagrams show you how to assemble the rhombic dodecahedron using four modules in each of three colours. Other colourings are, of course, possible and both designs also work well in just a single colour.

Folding the rhombic parallelogram module

Method 1

Whilst A4 paper is a fairly good approximation of a 1:√2 or silver rectangle it is not a completely mathematically accurate one. Method 1 will help you fold the module in the most accurate way. Use this method if you are folding all the modules yourself.

1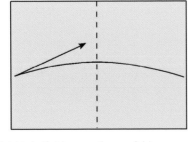
Fold in half sideways, then unfold.

2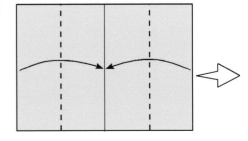
Fold the left and right edges into the centre.

3

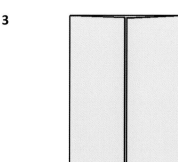

Turn over sideways.

4

Fold in half downwards

5

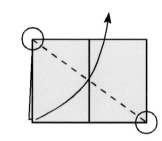

Fold the front layers in half diagonally upwards making sure both corners marked with circles become sharp points.

6

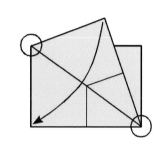

Open out the fold made in step 5.

7

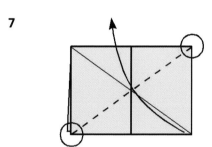

Fold the front layers in half diagonally upwards in the alternate direction making sure both corners marked with circles become sharp points.

8

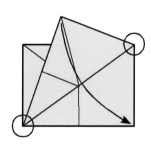

Open out the fold made in step 7.

9

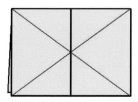

Turn over sideways.

10

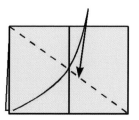

Repeat step 5 on the new front layers, then unfold.

11

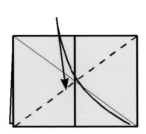

Repeat step 7 on the new front layers, then unfold.

12

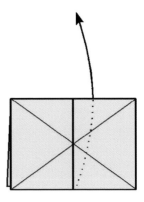

Open out upwards from behind.

13

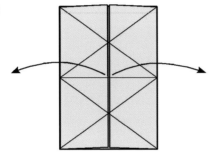

Open out the folds made in step 2.

14

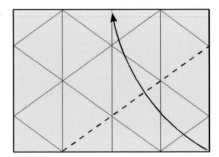

Check you have made all the creases shown here. Fold the bottom right corner inwards using the existing crease.

15

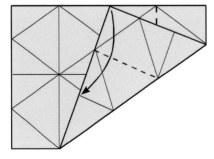

Make the fold shown by reversing the direction of the existing crease, then flatten to look like picture 16.

16

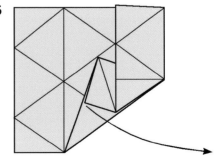

Open out the folds made in steps 14 and 15.

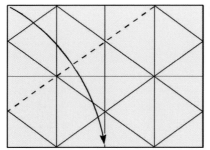

Fold the top left corner diagonally inwards using the existing crease.

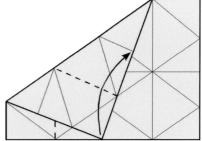

Make the fold shown by reversing the direction of the existing crease, then flatten to look like picture 19.

19

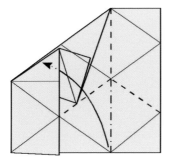

Refold the folds made in steps 14 and 15 underneath the front layer of the paper.

20

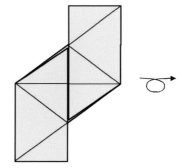

Turn over sideways.

21

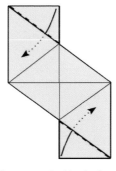

Tuck the flaps away inside the layers using the existing creases.

22

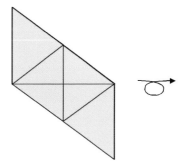

Turn over sideways.

23

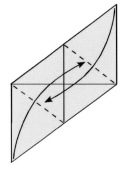

Fold both tabs inwards using the existing creases.

24

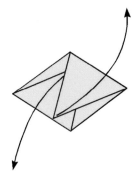

Open out the folds made in step 23 but do not flatten completely.

25

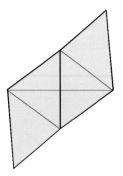

Turn over sideways.

26

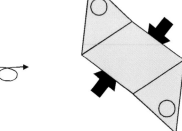

The basic rhombic parallelogram module is finished. Each module has two tabs (indicated by circles) and two pockets. Make twelve.

Method 2

This method will not produce quite such an accurate result (unless your paper is exactly 1:√2) but I always use it when teaching children to fold this module in a group as it is easier to understand and carry out. The modules will still go together sufficiently well to allow the rhombic dodecahedron to be constructed.

27

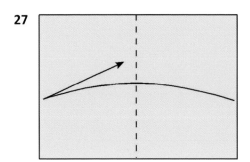

Fold in half sideways, then unfold.

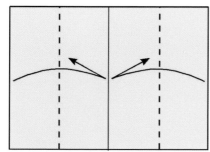

Fold the left and right edges into the centre, then unfold.

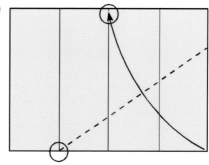

Fold the bottom right corner onto the centre of the top edge. If your paper is exactly 1:√2 the resulting crease will touch the bottom of the left hand quarter crease (marked with a circle). Since A4 paper is only an approximation of a 1:√2 rectangle your crease is unlikely to hit this point exactly. Don't worry too much about this.

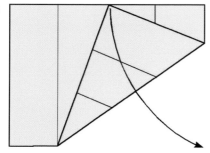

Open out the fold made in step 29.

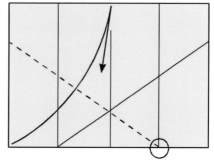

Fold the bottom left corner onto the centre of the top edge, then unfold.

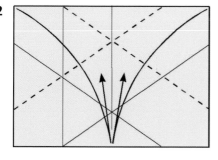

Fold both top corners in turn, then unfold, onto the centre of the bottom edge.

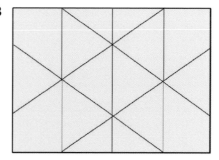

Now follow steps 14 through 19 so that the paper looks like picture 34.

34

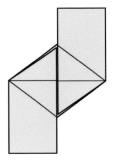

Turn over sideways, The next picture is on a larger scale.

35

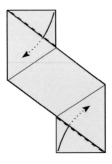

Fold the small single layer flaps at the top and bottom inwards over the edge of the other layers.

36

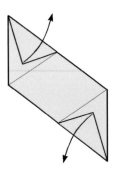

You can use the module like this but it is neater to first open out the folds made in step 41...

37

Fold the small single layer flaps at the top and bottom inwards over the edge of the other layers.

...and then tuck both flaps away in between the other layers.

38

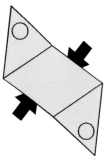

The basic rhombic parallelogram module is finished. Each module has two tabs (indicated by circles) and two pockets. Make twelve.

Putting the modules together

39

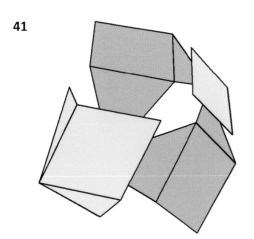

The tabs fit into the pockets on other modules like this.

40

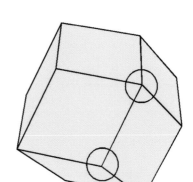

Four modules meet at each pointy corner. However only three modules meet at each of the flatter corners.

41

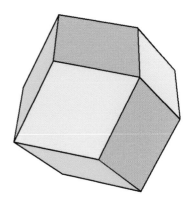

The first four modules go together like this. Once these are in place it is obvious, provided you understand the nature of the shape, how the others must be added.

42

The finished rhombic dodecahedron will look like this. You will find that it is a very robust shape and quite enjoyable to hold and play with.

Folding the rhombic triangle module

Begin by folding to step 16 of Method 1 (but do not open out fold 15).

43

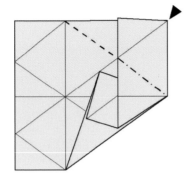

Turn the top right corner inside out in between the other layers using the existing creases.

44

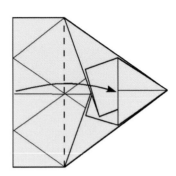

Fold the left edge inwards using the existing crease.

45

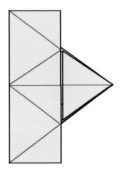

Turn over sideways.

46

Fold these two single layer flaps inwards in between the other layers.

47

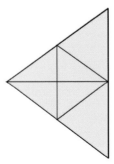

Turn over sideways.

48

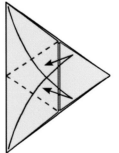

Fold the top and bottom left hand flaps inwards then unfold but do not flatten.

49

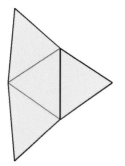

Turn over sideways.

50

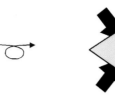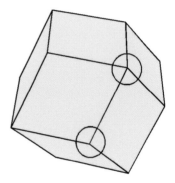

The rhombic triangle module is finished. This module also has two tabs (marked by circles) and two pockets. Make twelve.

51

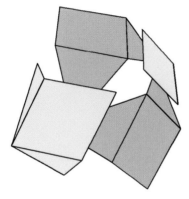

The first four modules go together like this. Once these are in place it is obvious, provided you understand the nature of the shape, how the others must be added.

52

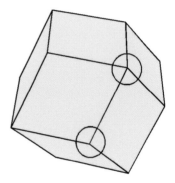

Four modules meet at each pointy corner. However only three modules meet at each of the flatter corners.

53

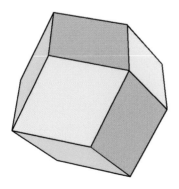

When finished this version of the rhombic dodecahedron is outwardly indistinguishable from the parallelogram module version.

Combining rhombic dodecahedra

Rhombic dodecahedra assembled from either type of module can be combined to create larger forms.

54

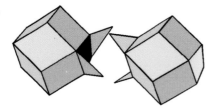

Two rhombic dodecahedra can be joined together by removing one module from each and reconfiguring the free tabs to point outwards rather than inwards.

55

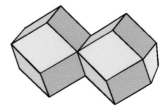

The result should look like this. If you make a second pair and turn them at right angles they will sit snugly on top of the first pair. Further pairs can be added to create a tower.

56

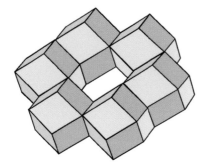

Alternatively, six rhombic dodecahedra can be arranged to form a ring.

57

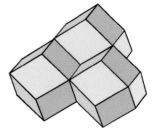

Three can be joined to create a honeycomb...

58

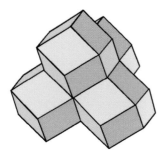

...and another added on top to create a pyramid.

59

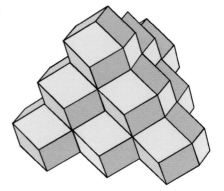

Larger pyramids with more layers are possible but the structure becomes weaker as more layers are added.

The Rhombic Tetrahedron

The rhombic tetrahedron has four faces each of which is a 70.32/54.84/54.84 degree triangle. This robust modular origami version can be made from two modules, each of which contributes two full faces to the form. The modules are mirror-images of each other and are each folded from a silver rectangle cut in half lengthwise, so that a complete rhombic tetrahedron can be obtained from a single silver rectangle.

A4 paper is a sufficiently close approximation of a silver rectangle to be used for this purpose. Alternatively a method of obtaining silver rectangles from US letter sized paper is given on pages 135 to 137.

The folding method is the same as that for the regular tetrahedron explained earlier in this book, except that it begins from a different paper shape. All the variations of the basic module that are possible for the regular tetrahedron are also possible for the rhombic tetrahedron. This folding method will generalise to any shape of rectangle.

Two rhombic tetrahedra will go together to form a rhombic pyramid, four to form a rhombic octahedron and twenty four to form a rhombic dodecahedron. Eight rhombic tetrahedra will go together to form a larger rhombic tetrahedron, thus proving that, unlike the regular tetrahedron, this shape will fill space.

Eight rhombic tetrahedra can also be joined together to form a rolling ring (see page 97)

These diagrams show you how to make a rhombic tetrahedron using modules of two different colours but the design also works well in a single plain colour.

Folding the modules

1

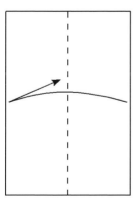

Fold a silver rectangle in half sideways, then unfold. When you have done this cut along the vertical crease to separate the two halves of the paper.

2

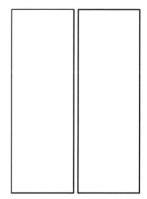

Either half of the paper can be used to fold a module from.

3

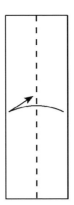

Begin with your paper arranged white side up. Fold in half sideways, then unfold.

4

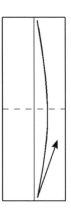

Fold in half downwards, then unfold.

5

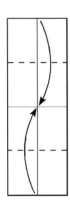

Fold both the top and bottom edges to the centre. The next picture is on a larger scale.

6

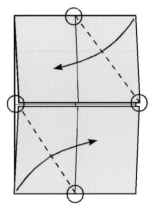

Fold the top right and bottom left corners inwards as shown, making sure that the creases begin and end at the points marked with circles. Accuracy is important here.

7

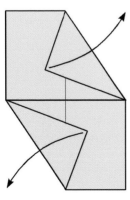

Unfold.

8

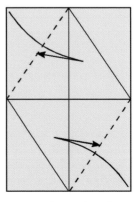

Repeat steps 6 and 7 on the other two corners.

9

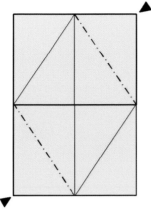

Turn the top right and bottom left corners inside out in between the other layers using the existing creases.

10

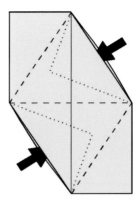

The pockets are marked with arrows. Configure the module to look like picture 11 by folding forwards along the three creases marked with dashed lines here.

11

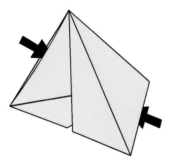

The first module is finished.

12

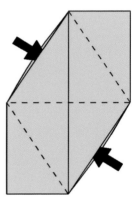

Fold a second module to step 9 but this time create pockets out of the top left and bottom right corners to create a mirror-image module. Configure to look like picture 13.

Putting the modules together

13

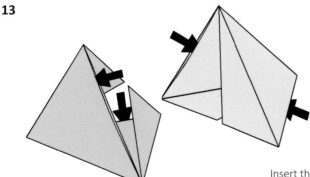

Insert the tabs of one module into the pockets of the other.

14

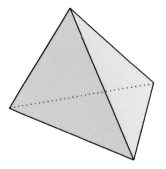

The finished rhombic tetrahedron should look like this.

15

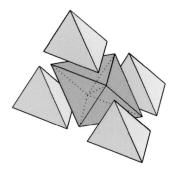

Just as you can make a large regular tetrahedron by stacking four small regular tetrahedra around a regular octahedron...

16

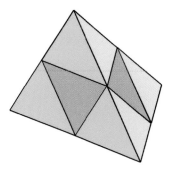

...so you can form a large rhombic tetrahedron by stacking four small rhombic tetrahedra around a rhombic octahedron.

17

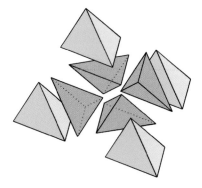

However, a rhombic octahedron can itself be made out of eight rhombic tetrahedra. This shows that, unlike regular tetrahedra, rhombic tetrahedra can fill space.

18

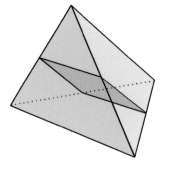

As the modular method demonstrates, the four faces of the rhombic tetrahedron are arranged in pairs which are formed from rhombs folded across their shorter axis. If you cut the rhombic tetrahedron into two equal halves through the centres of four of its edges - see diagram - the plane formed by the cut is also an identical rhomb. If you cut through the platonic tetrahedron in the same way the resulting plane is, of course, a square.

The Rhombic Hexahedron

Each of the faces of the rhombic hexahedron is a 109.28/70.32 rhombus. It can be made from either six rhombic parallelogram modules (see page 46) or six rhombic triangle modules (see page 54). In both cases the six modules must be folded in mirror-image pairs and, in order to allow the modules to fit together, one tab of each module must be truncated. Each module contributes one full face to the form.

Three rhombic hexahedra will go together to make a rhombic dodecahedron. If you want to hold them together in this form you can do so using the joining pieces explained on page 79.

A rhombic hexahedron can be built by combining three rhombic pyramids, six rhombic tetrahedra or twelve semi-rhombic tetrahedra.

Rhombic hexahedra will fill space.

These diagrams show you how to make a rhombic hexahedron using modules of three different colours but the design also works well in a single plain colour.

Begin by making six basic modules of whichever type you prefer to use and truncate one of the tabs of each module by following the instructions below. These diagrams show you how to truncate one tab of the basic rhombic parallelogram module but tabs of the rhombic triangle module can be truncated in exactly the same way.

Truncating tabs

1

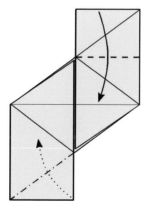

2

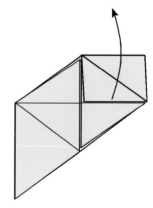

Begin by folding the modules to step 21 on page 49. Fold the small triangular flap at the bottom backwards in between the layers then fold the top edge downwards as shown.

Open out the fold made in step 1.

3

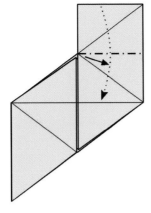

Pull the front right layers open, remake the fold made in step 1 in between the other layers and flatten again.

4

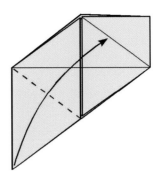

Fold the bottom left corner inwards using the existing crease.

5

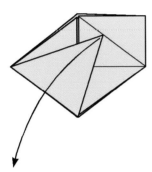

Open out the fold made in step 4.

6

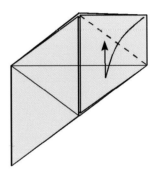

Fold the top right corner inwards, then unfold, using the existing crease.

7

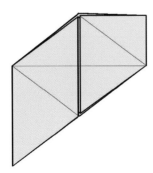

Turn over sideways.

8

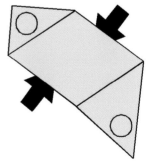

The singly truncated rhombic parallelogram module is finished.

Assembling the rhombic hexahedron from singly truncated rhombic parallelogram modules

9

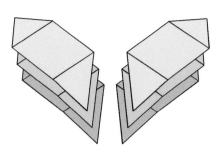

Make six singly truncated rhombic parallelogram modules. Three of these should be mirror images of the other three.

10

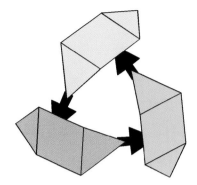

The first set of three modules go together like this.

11

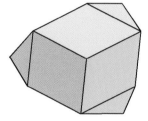

This is the front half of the design.

12

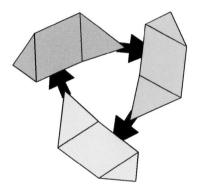

The second set of modules go together like this.

13

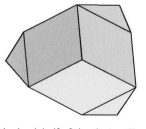

This is the back half of the design. Turn over sideways.

14

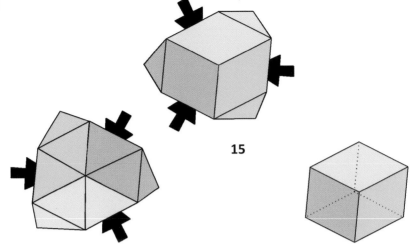

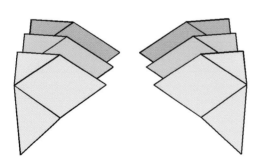

15

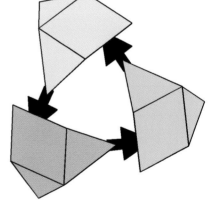

Attach the front half to the back half by inserting all the truncated tabs in their corresponding pockets.

The rhombic parallelogram module version of the rhombic hexahedron is finished.

Assembling the rhombic hexahedron from singly truncated rhombic triangle modules

16

17

Make six singly truncated rhombic parallelogram modules. Three of these should be mirror images of the other three.

The first set of three modules go together like this.

18

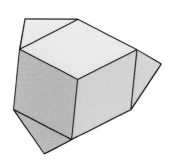

This is the front of the design.

19

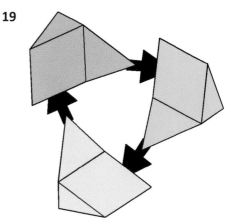

The second set of modules go together like this.

20

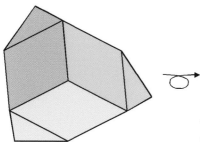

This is the back of the design. Turn over sideways.

21

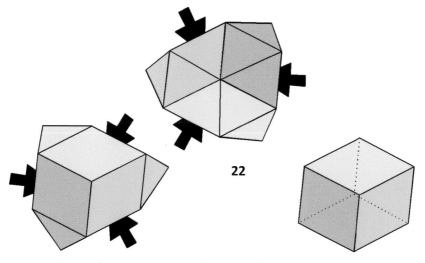

22

Attach the front to the back by inserting all the truncated tabs in their corresponding pockets.

This is the finished rhombic triangle version of the rhombic hexahedron. It is outwardly indistinguishable from the rhombic parallelogram module version.

The Rhombic Skew Cube

Like the rhombic hexahedron the rhombic skew cube also has six faces each of which is a 109.28/70.32 degree rhombus and can be made from two mirror-image sets of singly truncated rhombic parallelogram modules, each of which contributes one full face to the form. The modules used to make the rhombic hexahedron can be taken apart and used to make the rhombic skew cube.

A version made from rhombic triangle modules is also possible, but it does not hold together well unless a cut is introduced to separate the tabs.

Rhombic skew cubes will fill space but will not fit together to form a rhombic dodecahedron. You may like to add rhombic pyramids to the faces of a skew cube to see what the effect of this is.

These diagrams show you how to make a rhombic skew cube using modules of three different colours but the design also works well in a single plain colour.

1

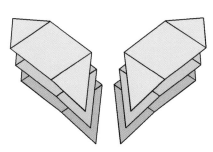

Begin by making six basic rhombic parallelogram modules (see pages 46 to 52) then truncate one of the tabs of each module by following steps 1 to 3 on pages 61 and 62. Three of these should be mirror images of the other three.

2

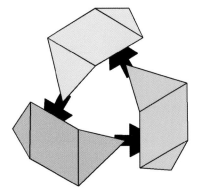

The first set of three modules go together like this.

3

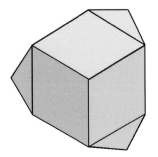

This is the front of the design.

4

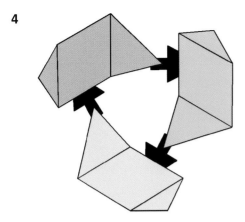

The second set of modules go together like this.

5

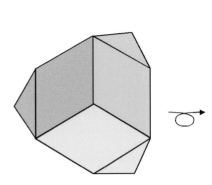

This is the back of the design. Turn over sideways.

6

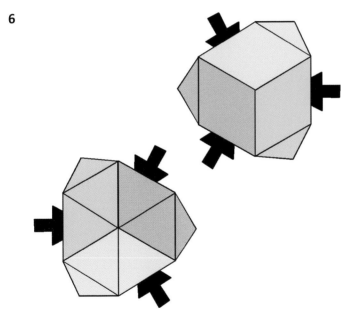

Attach the front to the back by inserting all the truncated tabs in their corresponding pockets.

7

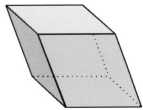

The rhombic skew cube is finished.

The Rhombic Octahedron

The rhombic octahedron has eight faces each of which is a 70.32/54.84/54.84 degree triangle. It can be made from four rhombic parallelogram modules or four rhombic triangle modules or a combination of the two. Each module contributes one full face to the form. It is much easier to assemble these designs if both tabs of the modules are truncated.

Six rhombic octahedra will go together to form a rhombic dodecahedron.

A rhombic octahedron can be made by combining two rhombic pyramids, two square-base semi-rhombic pyramids, four rhombic tetrahedra, or eight semi-rhombic tetrahedra.

Rhombic octahedra will fill space.

A rhombic octahedron can be combined with four rhombic tetrahedra to produce a larger compound rhombic tetrahedron. If both designs are folded starting from the same size of silver rectangle the faces of both will be the same size.

These diagrams show you how to fold the rhombic octahedron in two colours but the design also works well in just a single colour.

From four rhombic parallelogram modules

1

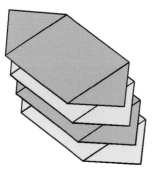

You will need four rhombic parallelogram modules, two in each of two colours, both tabs of which have been truncated in the way shown on pages 61 and 62. Begin by turning each module over and adding an extra crease in the way shown in step 2.

2

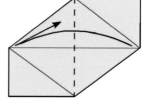

Fold in half sideways then unfold.

3

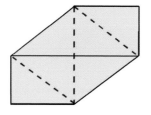

Configure the modules by folding them towards you along the lines marked with dashes here.

4

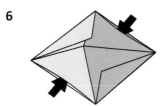

Begin by putting two modules together like this.

5

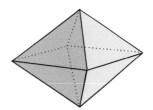

Turn the sub-assembly over sideways.

6

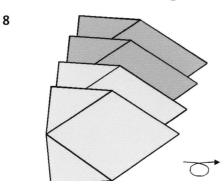

Make a second identical sub-assembly from the remaining two modules and add it to the front of the first sub-assembly like this.

7

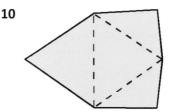

The finished rhombic octahedron should look like this.

From rhombic triangle modules

8

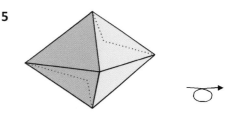

You will need four rhombic triangle modules, two in each of two colours, both tabs of which have been truncated in the way shown on pages 61 and 62. Begin by turning each module over and adding an extra crease in the way shown in step 9.

9

Fold in half sideways then unfold.

10

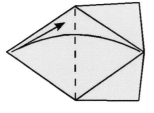

Configure the modules by folding them towards you along the lines marked with dashes here.

11

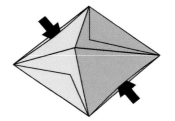

Begin by putting two modules together like this.

12

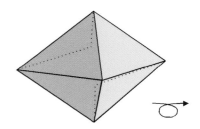

Turn the sub-assembly over sideways.

13

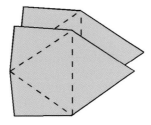

Make a second identical sub-assembly from the remaining two modules and add it to the front of the first sub-assembly like this.

14

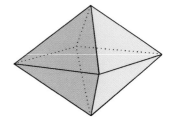

The finished rhombic octahedron should look like this.

From two mirror-image rhombic parallelogram modules and two rhombic triangle modules

15

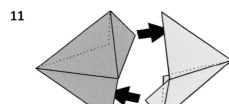

Configure the mirror-image rhombic parallelogram modules like this...

16

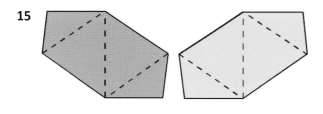

...and the rhombic triangle modules like this.

17

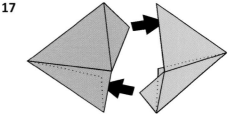

Begin by putting two modules together like this.

18

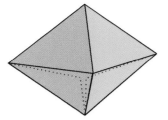

The resulting sub-assembly should look like this.

19

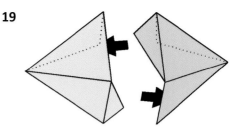

Put the other two modules together in a similar way to form a second sub-assembly.

20

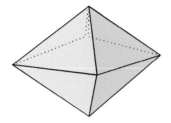

Turn this second sub-assembly over sideways.

21

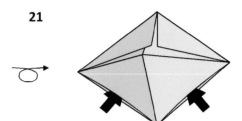

Add the first sub-assembly like this.

22

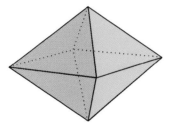

The rhombic octahedron is finished. There are several other ways to make a rhombic octahedron from rhombic modules which have their tabs and pockets arranged in other configurations. You may be interested in finding these for yourself.

Making a compound rhombic tetrahedron

23

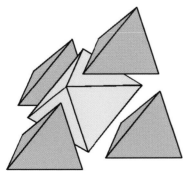

24

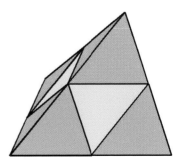

A rhombic octahedron can be combined with four rhombic tetrahedra to build a larger compound rhombic tetrahedron in the way shown here.

The Reoriented Rhombic Octahedron

A second kind of rhombic octahedron, which, for want of a better name, I call the reoriented rhombic octahedron, can be made from two mirror-image sets of two doubly truncated rhombic parallelogram modules. Other ways of making the same form using other combinations of rhombic triangle and parallelogram modules are possible.

Reoriented rhombic octahedra will not fill space and will not go together to make a rhombic dodecahedron.

1

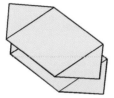

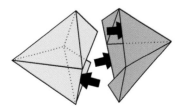

You will need four doubly truncated rhombic parallelogram modules in two mirror-image sets of two modules, both tabs of which have been truncated in the way shown on pages 61 and 62. Begin by turning each module over and adding an extra crease in the way shown in step 2.

2

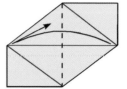

Fold in half sideways then unfold.

3

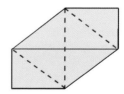

Configure the modules by folding them towards you along the lines marked with dashes here.

4

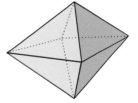

Put each set of modules together to form a sub-assembly then put the two sub-assemblies together like this.

5

When it is finished the reorientated rhombic octahedron will look like this. You will probably need to make a normal rhombic octahedron as well and sit them side by side to be able to fully appreciate the difference between these two forms.

The Rhombic Pyramid

The base of the rhombic pyramid is a 109.28/70.32 degree rhombus and each of its other four faces are 70.32/54.84/54.84 degree triangle. A modular origami version can be made in two parts, a base with four pockets and a 'hat' with four tabs, both of which are folded from the same size of silver rectangle. The base is a version of Nick Robinson's rhombic parallelogram module.

A4 paper is a sufficiently close approximation of a silver rectangle to be used for this purpose. Alternatively a method of obtaining silver rectangles from US letter sized paper is given on pages 135 and 136.

Two rhombic pyramids will go together to form a rhombic octahedron, three to form a rhombic hexahedron and twelve to form a rhombic dodecahedron. In the third edition of their classic book *Mathematical Models*, H M Cundy and A P Rollett (see inside back cover) state a Mr Dorman Luke, otherwise unknown to me, has found that all three stellations of the rhombic dodecahedron can be arrived at by adding rhombic pyramids to the rhombic dodecahedron.

In addition it is worth noting that four rhombic pyramids will go together to form a rhombic tetrahedron and eight to form a larger rhombic pyramid (thus proving that rhombic pyramids will fill space). Neither of these arrangements is immediately obvious when handling the pieces and both can therefore function as simple geometrical puzzles.

This section also includes diagrams for a simple joining piece which can be used to link rhombic pyramids, and other rhombic polyhedra, together into larger forms.

Folding the rhombic hat

1

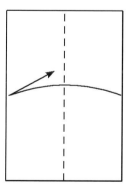

Begin with a silver rectangle. Fold in half sideways, then unfold.

2

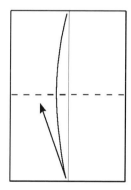

Fold in half from top to bottom, then unfold.

3

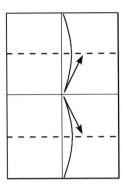

Fold the top and bottom edges into the centre, then unfold.

4

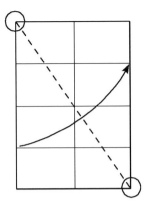

Fold the paper in half diagonally by bringing the point where the lower quarter way crease touches the left edge to the point where the upper quarter way mark touches the right edge. Adjust if necessary so that both corners marked with circles are sharp points.

5

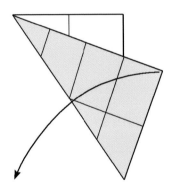

Unfold.

6

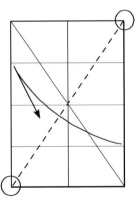

Repeat fold 4 in the alternative direction, then unfold.

7

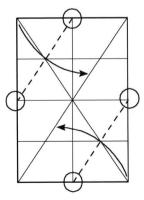

Fold the top right and bottom left corners inwards using the points marked with circles to locate the folds.

8

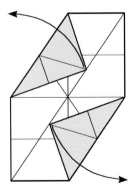

Unfold.

9

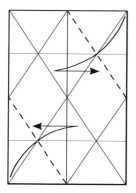

Fold the other two corners inwards in a similar way, then unfold.

10

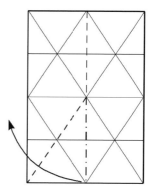

Fold the centre of the bottom edge diagonally to the left so that the design becomes three dimensional.

11

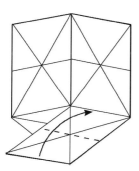

Fold the front edge inwards as shown so that the bottom layers flatten to look like picture 12.

12

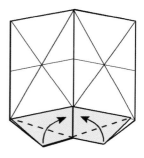

Fold both front flaps backwards to look like picture 13.

13

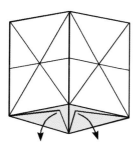

Unfold then open out completely.

14

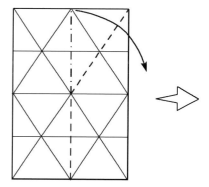

Repeat steps 10 through 13 on the upper half of the paper.

15

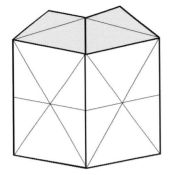

Remake folds 10 through 13 on the lower half of the paper. Making sure that the layers at the centre lie as flat as possible. Arrange the result to look like picture 16.

16

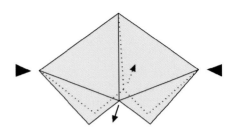

Crease all the outside edges firmly then squash flat sideways so that the paper looks like picture 17.

17

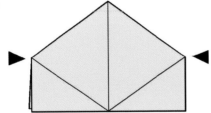

Crease the two top edges firmly, then press both sides inwards to open out to look like picture 18.

18

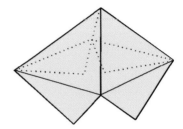

The rhombic hat is finished.

Folding the four pockets module

19

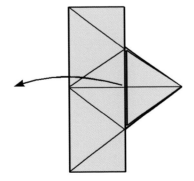

Begin by folding a silver rectangle of the same size you used to fold the rhombic hat to step 45 of the rhombic triangle module on page 54. Open out the front layer to the left.

20

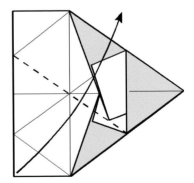

Fold the bottom left corner inwards along the line of the existing crease.

21

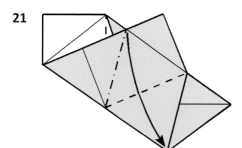

Fold the front layer in half downwards using the existing crease and flatten into the shape shown in picture 22.

22

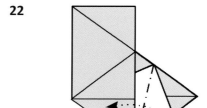

Fold the small triangular flap backwards so that it goes behind the two layers immediately below it using the existing crease.

23

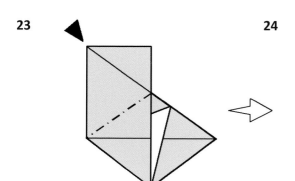

Turn the top left corner inside out in between the other layers using the existing crease. The next picture is on a larger scale.

24

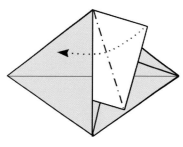

Repeat fold 4 on this second small triangular flap.

25

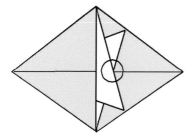

Tuck the flaps marked with a circle underneath the layer of paper which lies behind them.

26

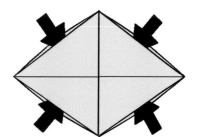

The four pockets module is finished.

Putting the modules together

27

28

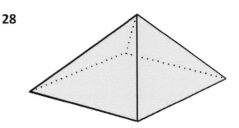

Sit the rhombic hat on top of the four pockets module and simply tuck all four tabs into the pockets below them. The result is a very robust rhombic pyramid that looks like this.

Two simple geometrical puzzles

Four rhombic pyramids can be arranged to form a rhombic tetrahedron and eight to form a larger rhombic pyramid. Neither of these arrangements is immediately obvious when handling the pieces and both can therefore function as simple geometrical puzzles. The solutions can be found on pages 142 and 143.

29

30

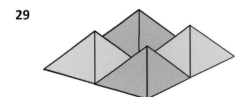

Four rhombic pyramids will go together to form a rhombic tetrahedron.

31

32

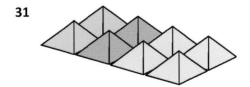
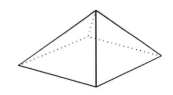

And eight, in three different ways, to make a larger rhombic pyramid.

Making a joining piece

If you want to link pyramids together more permanently to make other rhombic polyhedra you can do so using a simple joining piece made like this. This joining piece will not, however, work with the assembly puzzles.

33

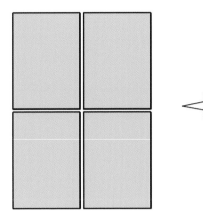

Each joining piece is made from a silver rectangle one quarter the size of the rectangle used to make the modules for the rhombic pyramid.

34

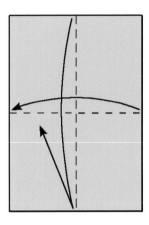

Fold in half downwards, then unfold. Also fold in half from right to left.

35

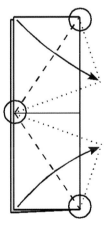

Fold the top and bottom left corners of the front layer diagonally to the right as shown. Make sure all the corners marked with circles remain or become sharp.

36

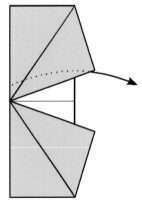

Fold the back layer across to the right behind the other layers. Picture 37 shows what the result should look like.

37

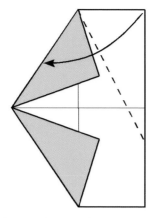

Fold the top edge onto the upper sloping left edge.

38

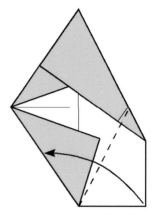

Fold the bottom edge onto the lower sloping left edge.

39

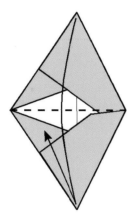

Fold in half downwards, then unfold.

40

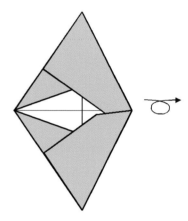

Turn over sideways.

41

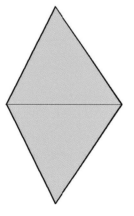

The joining piece is finished.

42

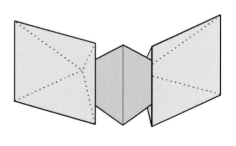

The joining piece can be used to link two pyramids, or other rhombic polyhedra, together like this.

The Semi-Rhombic Pyramid

The semi-rhombic pyramid has a square base and four faces which are 70.32/54.84/54.84 degree triangles. This modular origami version is made from four identical modules folded from silver rectangles, each of which contributes one triangular face and a quarter of the square base to the form.

A4 paper is a sufficiently close approximation of a silver rectangle to be used for this purpose. Alternatively a method of obtaining silver rectangles from US letter sized paper is given on pages 135 and 136.

Two semi-rhombic pyramids will go together to build a rhombic octahedron, six to build a cube and twelve, in several ways, to build a rhombic dodecahedron.

A semi-rhombic pyramid can be built from four semi-rhombic tetrahedra.

If you begin from a silver rectangle half the size of the one you used to make the rhombic dodecahedron the faces of both designs will be to the same scale.

Folding the modules

1

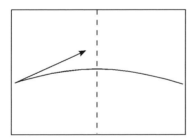

Begin with your paper arranged white side up. Fold in half sideways, then unfold.

2

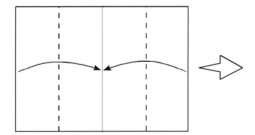

Fold both outside edges into the centre.

3

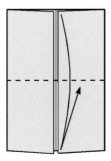

Fold in half downwards, then unfold.

4

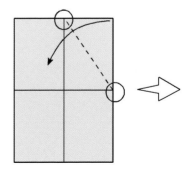

Fold the top right corner inwards making sure the new crease begins and ends at the points marked with circles.

5

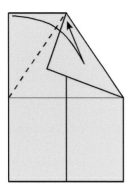

Fold the top left corner inwards in a similar way, then unfold.

6

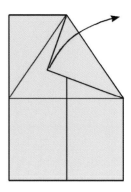

Open out the fold made in step 4.

7

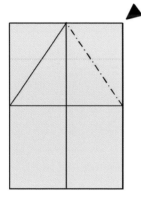

Turn the top right corner inside out in between the other layers using the existing creases.

8

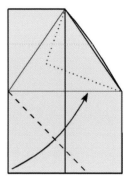

Fold the bottom left corner inwards using the horizontal centre crease to locate the fold.

9

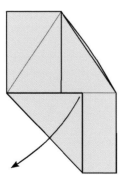

Unfold.

10

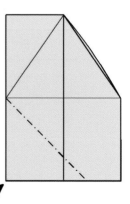

Turn the bottom left corner inside out in between the other folds using the existing creases.

11

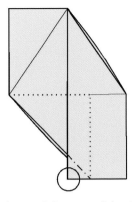

Fold the bottom left corner of the right front flap (marked with a circle) into the pocket behind it using the existing crease.

12

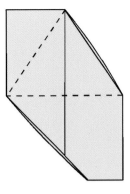

Configure the module by folding forwards along both the existing creases marked with dashed lines here.

13

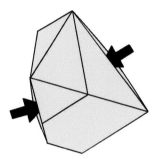

The finished module has two tabs and two pockets. Make all four.

Assembling the modules

14

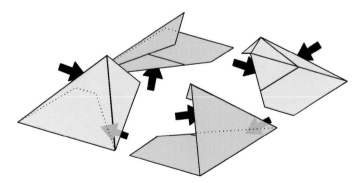

The four modules go together like this.

15

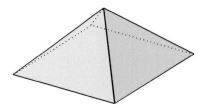

The semi-rhombic pyramid is finished.

The Square-Base Equilateral Pyramid

By varying the starting shape it is possible to achieve square-base pyramids of other proportions. You can, for instance, construct a square base pyramid with four equilateral faces by beginning from the double bronze rectangle (two bronze rectangles joined along their long edges) using the same modular method.

16

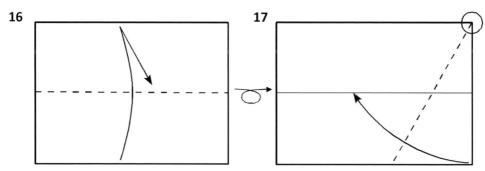

Begin with a sheet of A4 or US letter sized paper arranged white side up. Fold in half downwards, then unfold. Turn over sideways.

17

Fold the bottom right corner onto the horizontal centre crease, making sure that the crease starts from the top left corner, which becomes sharp.

18

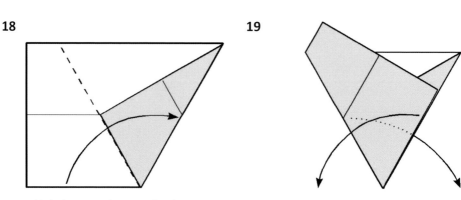

Fold the bottom edge onto the sloping right hand edge so that the bottom point becomes sharp.

19

Open out completely.

20

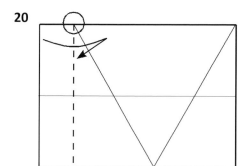

Fold the left edge inwards as shown, then unfold. Use the point where the crease made in step 19 meets the top edge to locate the fold. Accuracy is important here.

21

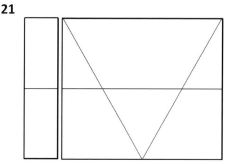

Cut along the crease made in step 20 to separate the two parts of the paper. The larger part is a double bronze rectangle.

22

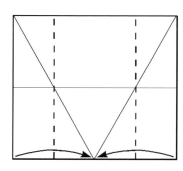

Fold both outside edges into the centre. Use the point where the sloping creases meet the bottom edge to locate these folds.

23

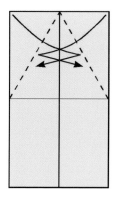

These two creases are already there in the front layers. Remake them through both layers then unfold.

24

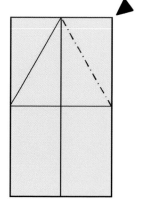

Continue with steps 7 through 14 of the instructions for the semi-rhombic pyramid, which are on pages 82 and 83.

25

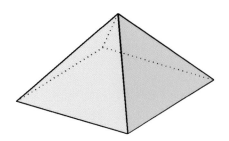

The finished square-base equilateral pyramid will look like this.

The Semi-Rhombic Tetrahedron

The semi-rhombic tetrahedron has one face that is a right angle isosceles triangle, one face that is a 70.32/54.84/54.84 degree triangle and two faces that are 90/54.84/35.16 degree triangles. This modular origami version is made from two silver rectangles, each of which is folded into a module of a different design.

The semi-rhombic tetrahedron can be used to build all the other rhombic and semi-rhombic polyhedra in this book. Two will go together to build a rhombic tetrahedron, four to build a semi-rhombic pyramid or a rhombic pyramid (in several ways), eight to build a rhombic octahedron, twelve to build a rhombic hexahedron and forty eight to build a rhombic dodecahedron.

If you begin from a silver rectangle one quarter the size of the one you used to make the rhombic dodecahedron the faces of both designs will be to the same scale.

Folding module one

1

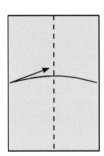

Fold in half sideways, then unfold.

2

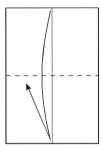

Fold in half downwards, then unfold.

3

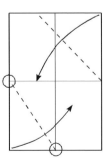

Fold the bottom left corner inwards making sure that the new crease begins and ends at the points marked with circles. Also fold in the top right corner as shown using the horizontal centre crease as a guide.

4

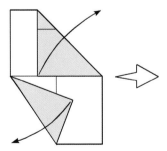

Open out both folds.

5

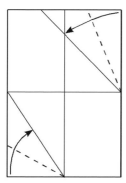

Fold the top half of the right edge and the left half of the bottom edge inwards to lie along the creases made in step 3.

6

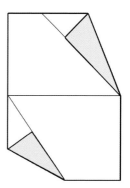

Repeat steps 3, 4 and 5 on the other two corners so that the result looks like picture 7.

7

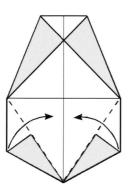

Fold both bottom corners inwards using the existing creases.

8

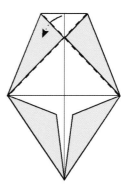

Lift both top corners up at right angles and tuck the central flap away inside the left hand pocket.

Folding module two

9

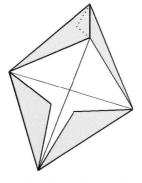

The result should look like this. Module one is finished.

10

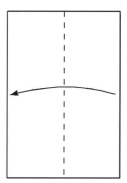

Fold in half sideways.

11

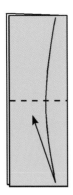

Fold in half upwards.

12

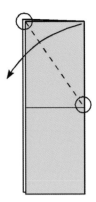

Fold the top right corner across to the left making sure that the new crease begins and ends at the points marked with circles and that the layers stay together as you do this.

13

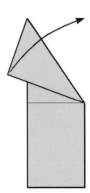

Unfold.

14

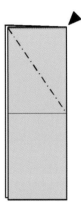

Turn the top right corner inside out in between the other layers using the existing creases.

15

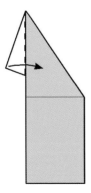

Fold the left corner of the middle layers across to the right along the line of the left edge of the front layer.

16

Repeat steps 12 to 15 on the lower half of the paper so that the result looks like picture 17.

17

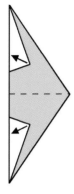

Lift the two front flaps up at right angles and configure the module by folding it forwards along the crease marked with a dashed line.

18

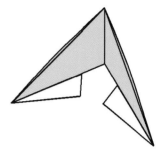

Module two is finished.

Putting the modules together

19

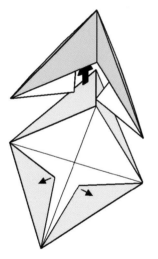

Arrange the two modules like this and insert the top of module one into the pocket in the bottom of module two.

20

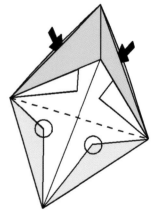

Insert the two flaps of module one into the two pockets at the top of module two.

21

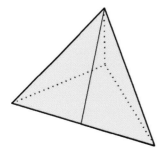

The semi-rhombic tetrahedron is finished.

The First Stellated Rhombic Dodecahedron

The first stellated rhombic dodecahedron has forty eight faces, all of which are 70.32/54.84/54.84 degree triangles. A first stellated rhombic dodecahedron can be made by adding twelve rhombic pyramids to the faces of a rhombic dodecahedron. Since a rhombic dodecahedron can itself be made by combining twelve rhombic pyramids it is clear that the volume of a first stellated rhombic dodecahedron is twice the volume of the underlying rhombic dodecahedron.

You can make a modular origami version using this method by adding rhombic hats (see pages 73 to 76) to rhombic parallelogram modules (see pages 46–52) and assembling the resulting compound modules in exactly the same way as the basic modules alone could be assembled into a rhombic dodecahedron (see page 53).

1

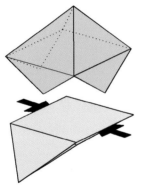

2

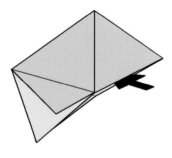

Begin by making twelve rhombic parallelogram modules and twelve rhombic hats. Add a rhombic hat to each rhombic parallelogram module by tucking two of the flaps at the bottom of the hat into the pockets of the rhombic parallelogram module to form a sub-assembly.

Each sub-assembly will look like this. Make all twelve then put them together in exactly the same way as the rhombic dodecahedron (see page 53). Because of the extra weight of the hats the assembly is not as robust as the underlying rhombic dodecahedron and will need to be picked up and handled with care.

Alternatively, the first stellated rhombic dodecahedron can be made using six modules which fit together in much the same way as the famous burr puzzle version of this shape, but without the central pyramids, which makes the assembly process less challenging.

Each module is folded from a 1:√2 or silver rectangle. A4 paper is a sufficiently close approximation of a silver rectangle to be used for this purpose. Alternatively a method of obtaining silver rectangles from US letter sized paper is given on pages 135 and 136.

The first stellated rhombic dodecahedron will fit inside the faces of a cube.

First stellated rhombic dodecahedra will fill space.

These diagrams show you how to make a first stellated rhombic dodecahedron using three sets of two modules in different colours but the design also works well in just a single colour.

Folding the modules

1
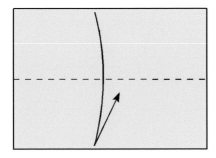

Begin with a silver rectangle arranged coloured side up. Fold in half downwards, then unfold.

2

Turn over sideways.

3
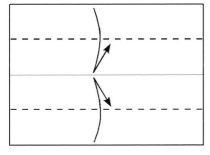

Fold the top and bottom edges onto the horizontal crease, then unfold.

4
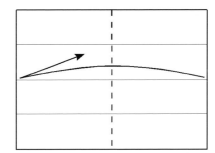

Fold in half sideways, then unfold.

5

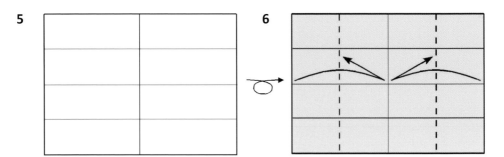

Turn over sideways.

6

Fold both outside edges onto the vertical crease, then unfold.

7

Fold in half from left to right using the existing crease.

8

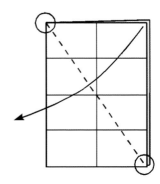

Fold the top right corner of the front layer inwards as shown, making sure the crease is formed accurately between the two points marked with circles.

9

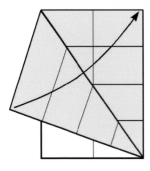

Unfold.

10

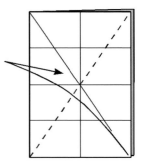

Repeat step 9 on the bottom right corner of the front layer, then unfold.

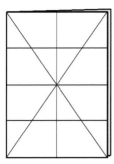

Turn over sideways.

12

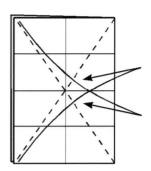
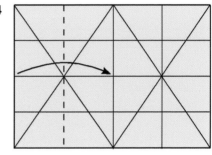

Repeat steps 9 and 10 on the other half of the paper.

13

Open out.

14

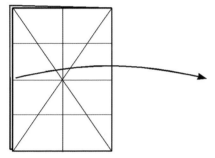

Fold the left edge inwards using the existing crease.

15

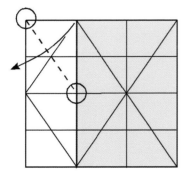

Fold the top right corner of the front layer outwards as shown, making sure the crease is formed accurately between the two points marked with circles.

16

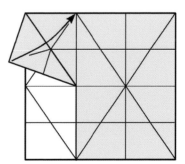

Unfold.

17

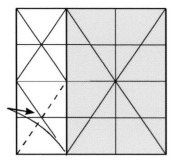

Fold the bottom right corner of the front layer outwards in a similar way, then unfold.

18

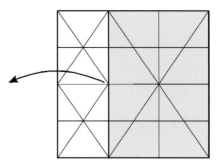

Open out, then repeat steps 14 through 17 on the other half of the paper.

19

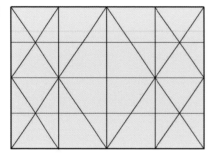

The result should look like this. Check you have made all the creases shown then turn over sideways.

20

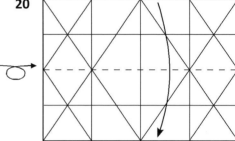

Fold in half downwards, reversing the direction of the existing crease.

21

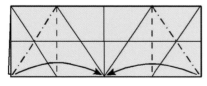

Fold the bottom left and right corners of the front layer into the centre. Make the same folds in the back layer at the same time so that if you were to turn the paper over it would look exactly the same at the back as at the front.

22

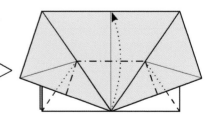

Fold the bottom edge of the front layers backwards inside the other layers and flatten to look like picture 23. Make the same folds in the back layer at the same time so that if you were to turn the paper over it would look exactly the same at the back as at the front.

23

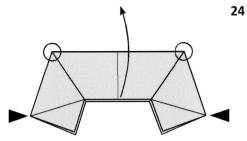

The result should look like this. Make sure all the folds lie flat inside the corners marked with circles. Open the bottom edge of the front layers out upwards and squash to look like picture 24.

24

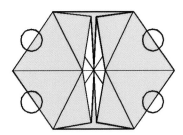

Make new creases along the edges marked with circles by flattening the edges firmly.

25

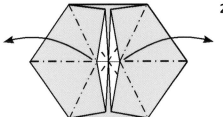

Open out the centres of the front layers as shown. The module will become three-dimensional as you do this.

26

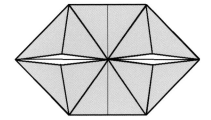

This is what the finished module should look like from below.

27

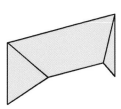

From the side it should look like this. Make six, two in each of three contrasting but complementary colours.

28

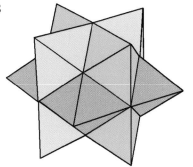

Six modules will go together like this to form the finished stellated rhombic dodecahedron. There are no tabs and no pockets. The modules wrap around each other to hold each other in place.

Other Convex Rhombic Polyhedra

There are (at least) five other convex polyhedra which can be made from rhombic parallelogram modules. These are analogues of the five polyhedra shown below, which we have already encountered and which are made from equilateral modules.

Substituting the rhombic parallelogram module for the equilateral module does not change the modular method (so the instructions will still work) but does, of course, change the proportions of the designs.

You may like to make up a set of ten modules, which is sufficient for all these designs, and make them for yourself. Once you have made one of the designs the modules can be taken apart and re-used to make the next.

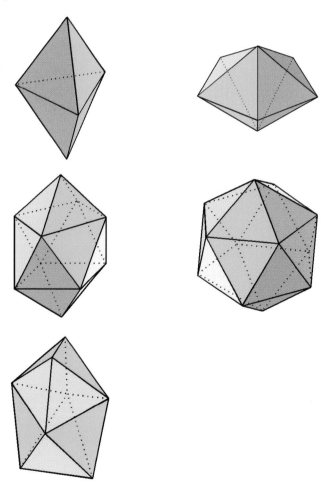

Rolling Ring of Eight Rhombic Tetrahedra

If eight rhombic tetrahedra are linked together in a circle by their long edges the result is a ring that will rotate through its centre of symmetry. This modular origami version is made from four modules. Half of each module goes outside a second module and half goes inside a third, so that the modules are effectively woven together.

Each module is folded from a 1:√2 or silver rectangle. A4 paper is a sufficiently close approximation of a silver rectangle to be used for this purpose. Alternatively a method of obtaining silver rectangles from US letter sized paper is given on pages 135 and 136.

Folding the modules

1

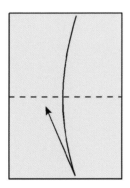

Fold in half downwards, then unfold.

2

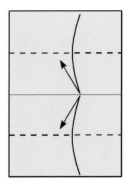

Fold the top and bottom edges into the centre, then unfold.

3

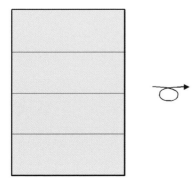

Turn over sideways.

4

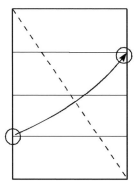

Fold the point where the bottom quarter way crease intersects the left edge onto the point where the top quarter way crease intersects the right edge. In theory, the resulting crease should pass through both the top left and bottom right corners. Adjust the position of this crease slightly if necessary so that it does so.

5

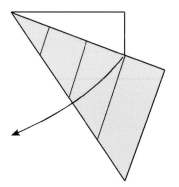

Unfold.

6

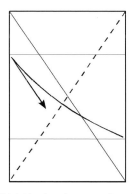

Repeat fold 4 in the alternate direction.

7

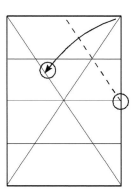

Fold the top right corner onto the diagonal crease, making sure the crease begins from the point marked with a circle.

8

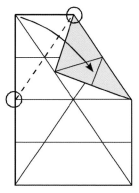

Fold the top left corner inwards in a similar way making sure the crease begins and ends at the points marked with circles.

9

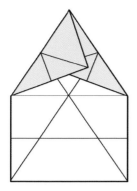

Repeat folds 7 and 8 on the lower half of the paper.

10

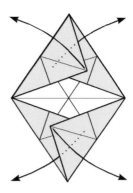

Unfold completely.

11

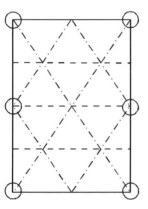

Bring each pair of circled points together in front so that, if you have remembered to turn your paper over after step 3, your paper collapses into the shape shown in picture 12.

12

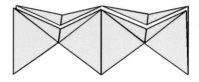

The first module is finished. Make all four.

Putting the modules together

13

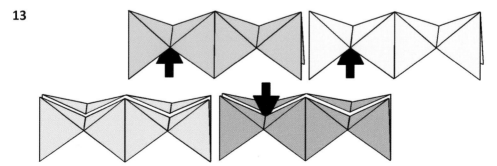

Put the modules together like this. Note that the top modules are arranged upside down and that half of each module goes inside, and half outside, the modules on either side.

14

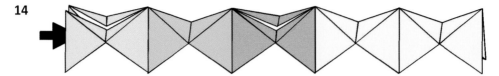

The result should be a caterpillar-like form like this. Curl the model up and insert half the yellow module inside the blue module.

15

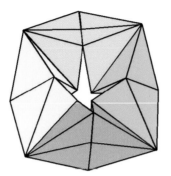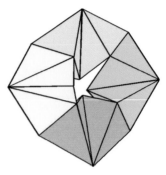

Make sure the modules nest accurately together. The rolling ring of eight rhombic tetrahedra is finished. The tetrahedra will rotate through the centre of the ring. After a few rotations the folds will settle down and the ring will turn without effort.

The
Triacontahedron

The Triacontahedron

The triacontahedron has thirty faces, each of which is a 116.34/63.26 rhombus. Fortunately for the modular origami designer a suitable module which produces faces of this shape can be obtained from the golden rectangle by using the same folding sequence that we have already used to obtain the basic equilateral and rhombic modules.

As far as I am aware the first person to construct such a design was the British paperfolder Jonathan Shapcott.

Golden rectangles can be made from A4 or US letter sized paper by following the instructions on pages 138 to 140. The folding method for the template is mathematically accurate but, because of the inaccuracies likely to be introduced during the folding process, it is a good idea to check that the first sheet folded from the template is an accurate golden rectangle before folding all the others. A way of doing this by folding alone is given on page 104. Adjust the template as necessary to produce golden rectangles as accurately as you can.

These diagrams show you how to make a triacontahedron using six modules in each of five colours. Other colourings are possible.

Because the angles between the faces are shallow the finished triacontahedron is not as stable as many of the designs in this book and so requires more careful handling. It will happily stand on a table to be looked at but, unless glued together, will not withstand being passed around a classroom. Stability is increased if the modules are made from smaller sheets of paper.

Folding the modules

1

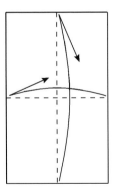

Fold your first golden rectangle in half edge to edge, then unfold, in both directions.

2

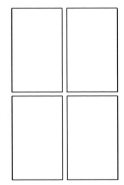

Cut along the crease lines to separate your paper into quarters. Each of these quarters is, of course, also a golden rectangle. Fold one of these quarter-size golden rectangles into a module following the folding sequence for the basic equilateral module (steps 1 through 16 on pages 18 to 21).

3

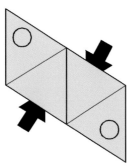

The finished module has two tabs (marked by circles) and two pockets (indicated by arrows). Make six in each of five colours.

4

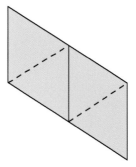

Configure the modules by folding towards you along the lines marked with dashed lines.

Putting the modules together

5

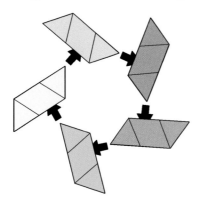

The first five modules go together in a ring, like this.

6

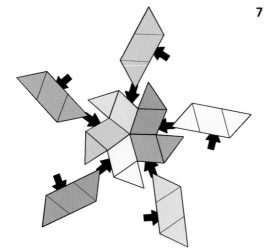

Add five more modules like this. Continue to add modules until the design is complete, keeping to the colour scheme shown.

7

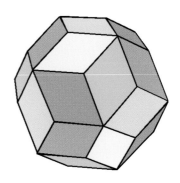

The finished triacontahedron will look like this.

How to check if your paper is an accurate golden rectangle

1

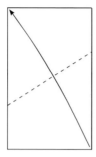

Fold the bottom right corner onto the top left corner.

2

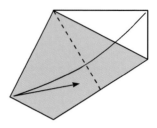

Fold the top right corner onto the left corner, then unfold.

3

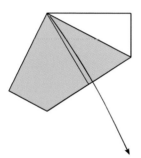

Open out.

4

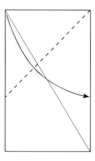

You should now have a diagonal crease running between the top left and bottom right corners. Check that this crease has been made accurately and adjust if necessary. When you have done this fold the top edge onto the right edge.

5

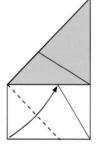

Fold the left edge onto the bottom edge of the front layer.

6

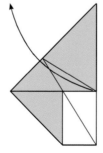

Open out the fold made in step 4.

7

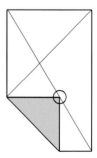

If your paper is an accurate golden rectangle the top right corner of the front layer will sit on the diagonal crease made in step 2.

Planar Polyhedra

The Planar Cube

The planar cube consists of twelve 70.32/54.84/54.84 degree triangular planes and can be modelled using twelve modules, each of which contributes one representation of a plane to the form. Each of the modules is very simple and is folded from a 1:√2 or silver rectangle. A4 paper is a good enough approximation of a silver rectangle to be used for this purpose. If you do not have access to A4 paper a method of obtaining silver rectangles from US letter sized paper is given on pages 135 and 136. The ideal size of paper to use for this design is probably one quarter A4. This method of making a planar cube was first discovered by the British paperfolder David Brill.

The planar cube is not a particularly stable or robust design, although it will hold together when sat on a table top and withstand gentle handling. If you want to pass it around a classroom it is best to glue the modules together, although doing this makes it impossible to add planar tetrahedra inside the design.

The method of folding the modules will generalise to other rectangles. The Japanese paperfolder Kunihiko Kasahara has, for instance, shown that beginning with a golden, rather than a silver, rectangle produces a module that will make a planar icosahedron.

These diagrams show you how to make a planar cube using four modules in each of three colours but the design also works well in just a single colour. Other colourings are possible.

Folding the modules

1

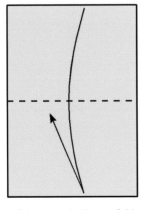

Fold in half downwards, then unfold.

2

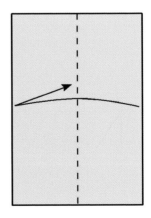

Fold in half sideways, then unfold.

3

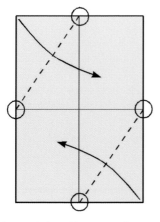

Fold the top left and bottom right corners inwards making sure that your creases begin and end at the points marked with circles. Accuracy is important here.

4

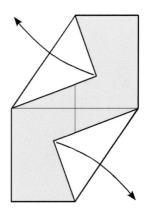

Unfold.

5

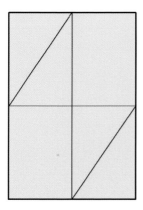

Turn over sideways.

6

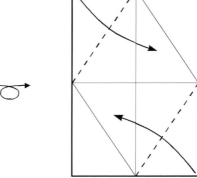

Repeat step 3 on the other two corners.

7

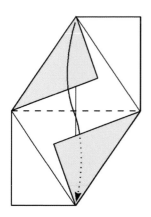

Fold the paper in half downwards using the existing crease, interlocking the two internal flaps as you do so.

8

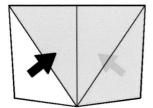

The module is finished. It has two tabs and two pockets, which are marked with arrows here. Make all twelve modules.

Putting the modules together

9

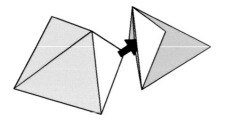

The first two modules go together like this.

10

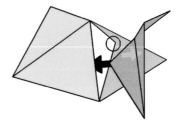

You can add a third module like this to complete one vertex of the cube. The tab marked with a circle slides inside the pocket marked with a grey arrow.

11

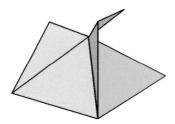

The three module assembly looks like this. The best strategy for assembling the whole design is to begin by using four modules to create an upside down square based pyramid, to add four more modules to create four vertexes and then to add the remaining four modules at the top.

12

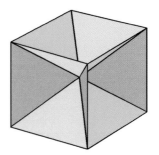

The planar cube is finished.

> **You can add either one or two planar tetrahedra to this design. See page 112. Adding a planar tetrahedron greatly improves the stability of the design. Adding two makes it much more stable still.**

The Planar Tetrahedron

The planar tetrahedron consists of six 109.68/35.16/35.16 degree triangular planes and can be modelled using six modules, each of which contributes a representation of one plane to the form. Each of the modules is very simple and is folded from a 1:√2 or silver rectangle. A4 paper is a good enough approximation of a silver rectangle to be used for this purpose. If you do not have access to A4 paper a method of obtaining silver rectangles from US letter sized paper is given on pages 135 and 136. The ideal size of paper to use for this design is probably one quarter A4.

The planar tetrahedron is somewhat challenging to put together and needs to be handled delicately during the assembly stage. However, once fully assembled, it becomes much stronger. If you want a completely robust model you will need to glue the modules together.

The diagrams show you how to make a planar tetrahedron using two modules in each of three colours but the design also works well in just a single colour.

Folding the modules

1

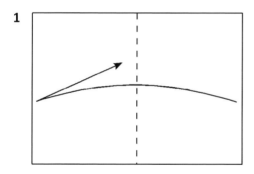

Fold in half sideways, then unfold.

2

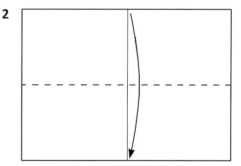

Fold in half downwards.

3

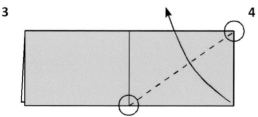

Fold both layers of the bottom right corner diagonally upwards as shown, making sure that the crease begins and ends at the points marked with circles.

4

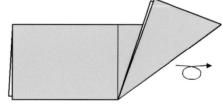

Turn over sideways.

5

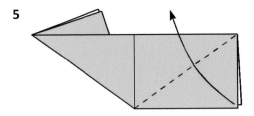

Repeat fold 3 on the new bottom right corner.

6

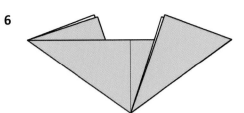

Open out completely.

7

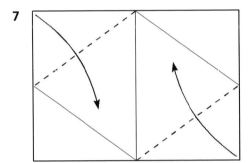

Fold the top left and bottom right corners inwards using the existing creases.

8

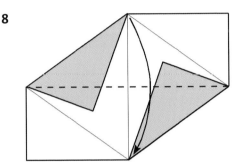

Fold in half downwards using the existing crease. Make this crease through all the layers.

9

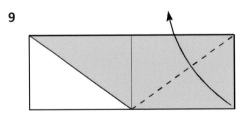

Fold the front bottom right corner upwards using the existing crease.

10

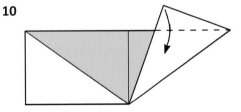

Fold the top corner of the front flap downwards along the line of the folded edge behind it.

11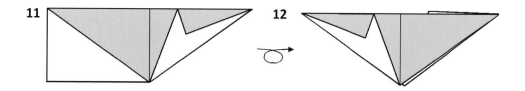

Turn over sideways and repeat steps 9 and 10 on the other side.

12

The module is finished. Open both flaps up to about 120 degrees. Make all six.

13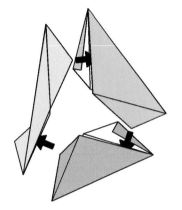

The first three modules go together like this.

14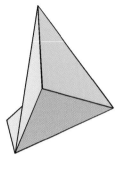

Rest this pyramid on a flat surface and add the remaining three modules to complete the assembly.

15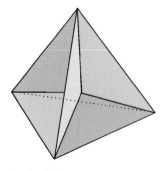

The finished planar tetrahedron should look like this.

Adding Planar Tetrahedra to the Planar Cube

The relationship between the cube and the regular tetrahedron can be simply and effectively demonstrated by adding either one or two planar tetrahedra to a planar cube.

In all cases all the modules for all the shapes must be folded from the same size of silver rectangles. A4 paper is a good enough approximation of a silver rectangle for this purpose. If you do not have access to A4 paper a method of obtaining a silver rectangle from US letter sized paper is given on pages 135 and 136. The ideal size of paper to use is probably one quarter A4.

Ian Harrison first came up with the idea of adding a planar tetrahedron to a planar cube in this way.

Adding a single Planar Tetrahedron to a Planar Cube

1

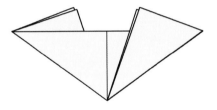

Begin by folding six silver rectangles to step 6 of the planar tetrahedron (see page 110)

2

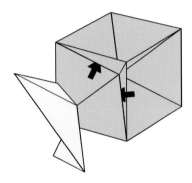

Add the first module to the planar cube assembly by inserting the tabs into the pockets marked with arrows here.

3

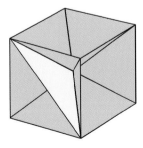

The first module is in place. Add the other five in the same way.

4

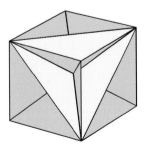

A single planar tetrahedron has been added to the planar cube. The original planar cube should be much more stable now.

Adding two Planar Tetrahedra to a Planar Cube

You will need twelve silver rectangles for the modules used to make the planar tetrahedra, of the same size as the silver rectangles used to make the planar cube, and six more, of half the size of the others, to fold into joining pieces. In order to be able to easily distinguish one planar tetrahedron from the other use paper of a different colour for the modules for each. The joining pieces can be made from any colour paper as they are not visible once the design is fully assembled.

1

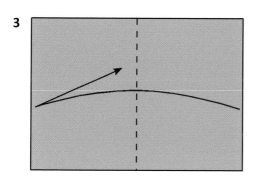

Fold all twelve modules for the planar tetrahedra to step 6 of the planar tetrahedron (see page 110). Six should be in one colour and the other six in another.

2

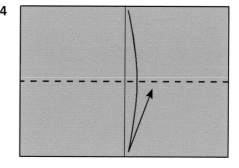

Cut each module into two along the vertical centre crease like this.

Folding the joining pieces

3

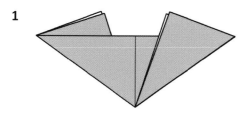

Use silver rectangles half the size of the ones you used to fold the modules for the planar tetrahedra. Fold in half sideways, then unfold.

4

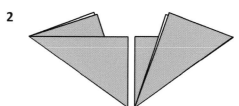

Fold in half downwards, then unfold.

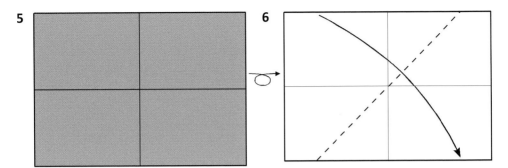

5 Turn over sideways.

6 Fold in half diagonally as shown making sure that your crease passes through the centre of the paper and that when the fold has been made the creases line up at the places marked with circles on picture 7.

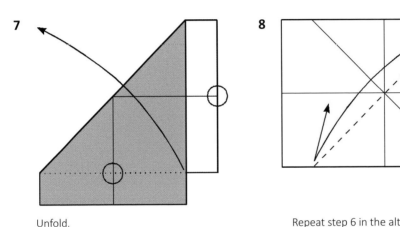

7 Unfold.

8 Repeat step 6 in the alternate direction, then unfold.

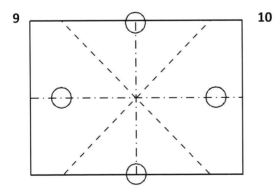

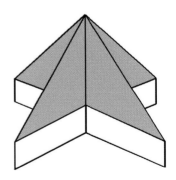

9 Bring the four points marked with circles together in front so that the centre moves away from you.

10 Arrange the resulting form to look like this. The joining piece is finished. Make six.

11

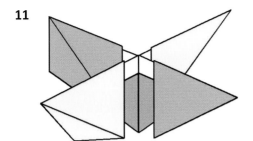

Slide four of the modules onto the arms of a joining piece to form a sub-assembly like this. Make six.

12

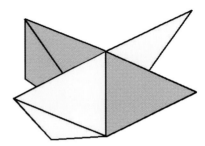

Drop the first sub-assembly into the open top of the planar cube and tuck all four tabs into the pockets underneath them.

13

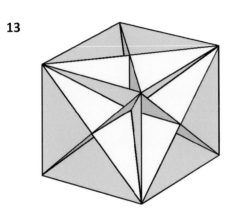

Add the remaining sub-assemblies in a similar way. The planar cube with two planar tetrahedra is finished.

Six Intersecting Planes in a Cube

The combination of two planar tetrahedra with a planar cube can also be seen as a compound of six intersecting planes, each of which is a silver rectangle. In order to show this you will need to fold two modules in each of six colours for the planar cube and two in each of six colours (which will then be cut in half to make four modules) for the two planar tetrahedra.

1

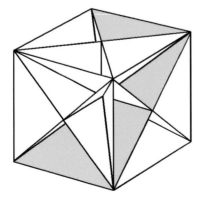

One plane of the form is made out of six modules of the same colour like this.

2

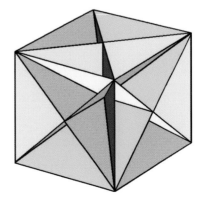

The finished design will look like this.

The Planar Octahedron

The planar octahedron can be seen as being composed of three intersecting or interpenetrating square planes. It can be modelled using six very simple modules folded from squares. Pages 128 and 129 show you how to make squares from A4 or US letter sized paper. The design is a little fiddly to put together but very robust once the modules have been persuaded to settle into place.

The planar octahedron was first discovered by the American paperfolder Robert E Neale.

These diagrams show you how to make a planar tetrahedron using two modules in each of three colours. Other colourings are possible.

Folding the modules

1

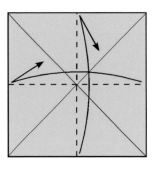

Fold in half diagonally, then unfold, in both directions.

2

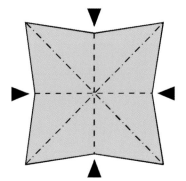

Turn over sideways.

3

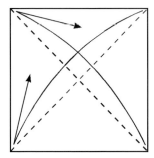

Fold in half edge to edge, then unfold, in both directions.

4

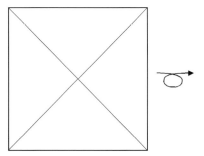

Collapse using the existing creases so that the centre moves towards you.

5

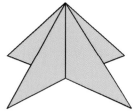

The finished module should look like this. Make two in each of three colours.

Putting the modules together

6

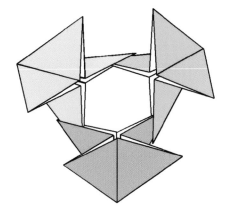

The first three modules go together like this.

7

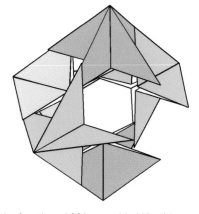

The fourth and fifth are added like this...

8

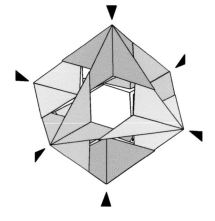

...and the last one like this. Gently nudge the modules together by opposite corners and opposite edges until the modules settle firmly into place and there is no longer a hole at the centre.

9

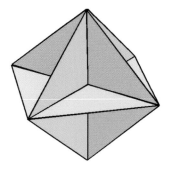

When it is finished the planar octahedron should look like this.

The Planar Cuboctahedron

The planar cuboctahedron can be seen as being composed of four intersecting hexagonal planes. It can be modelled by using twenty four modules, each of which is folded from a 2:√3 rectangle. A rectangle of these proportions is easily obtained by cutting a bronze rectangle in half. A method of easily obtaining bronze rectangles from A4 or US letter sized paper is given on pages 130 and 131.

These diagrams show you how to make a planar cuboctahedron using six modules in each of four colours so that each hexagonal plane is coloured independently. Other colourings are, of course, possible.

Folding the modules

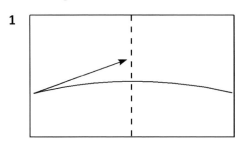

1

Begin with a bronze rectangle. Fold it in half sideways, then unfold.

2

Cut your rectangle in half along the vertical centre crease.

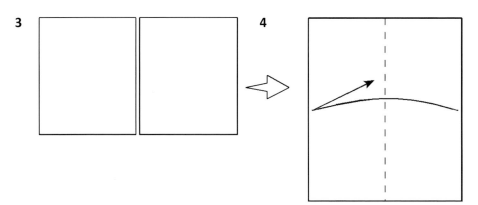

3

Each of the resulting rectangles can be folded into a module. The next picture is on a larger scale.

4

Fold in half sideways, then unfold.

5

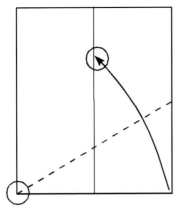

Fold the bottom right corner onto the vertical centre crease, making sure the crease begins from the bottom left corner, which becomes sharper.

6

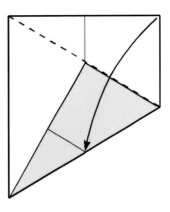

Fold the top right corner inwards in a similar way.

7

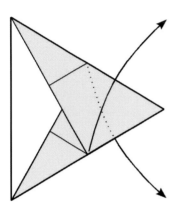

Undo the folds made in steps 5 and 6.

8

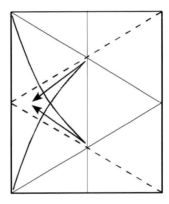

Repeat folds 5 and 6 on the two remaining corners, then unfold.

9

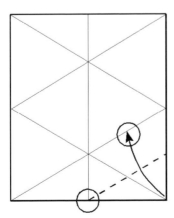

Fold the bottom right corner onto the crease made in step 5, making sure the crease begins from the centre of the bottom edge.

10

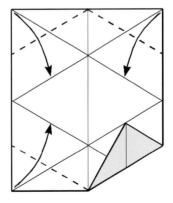

Fold the three remaining corners inwards in a similar way.

11

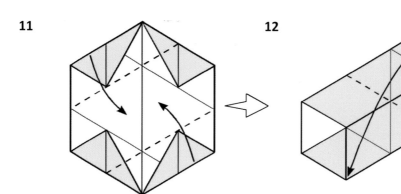

Fold the top left and bottom right sloping edges inwards using the existing creases.

12

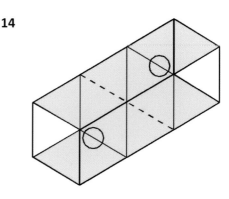

Fold in half diagonally, like this.

13

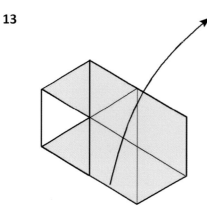

Unfold.

14

Remake the fold made in step 12 but this time interweave the flaps marked with circles as you do so.

15

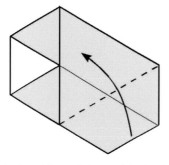

The back and front of the module should now be locked together. Fold the bottom right edge of the module inwards as shown.

16

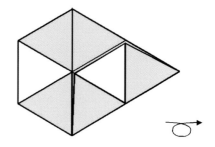

Turn over sideways.

17

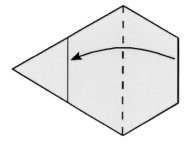

Fold the right edge inwards in a similar way.

18

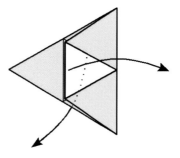

Unfold the tabs created in steps 15 and 16.

19

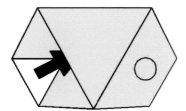

The first module is finished. It has a tab and a pocket at the front and another set at the back. Make all twenty four.

Putting the modules together

20

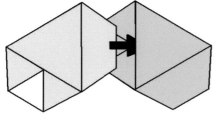

Slide the right hand tab of the first module into the left hand pocket of the second.

21

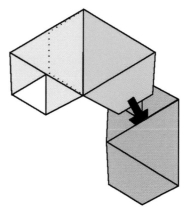

Make sure the left hand tab of the second module, which is at the back, has NOT been inserted into the corresponding pocket of the first module. Add a third module in a similar way.

22

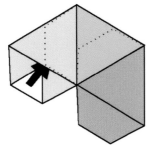

Complete a three-sided ring by inserting the bottom tab of the third module inside the left hand pocket of the first.

23

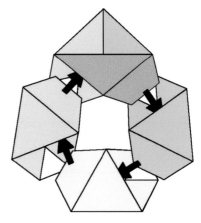

Add three more modules in a similar way to create a four-sided ring.

24

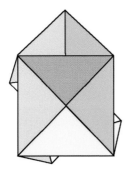

Continue to add modules until the planar cuboctahedron is complete. You will notice that four modules meet at each vertex. Make sure that when you add the final module to complete a vertex all the tabs of all the modules are securely tucked into their corresponding pockets. This design is not completely stable during assembly but will become more robust when it is complete.

25

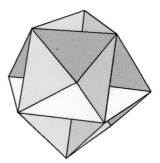

The finished planar cuboctahedron should look like this. If you have followed the colour scheme correctly the design will look as though it is composed of four interpenetrating hexagonal planes.

The Planar Icosidodecahedron

The planar icosidodecahedron can be seen as composed of six interpenetrating decagonal planes. Each of the sixty modules required to construct this form is folded from a square using what I call mock platinum folding geometry, which approximates the angles required sufficiently closely that the design will work. Pages 128 and 129 show you how to make squares from A4 or US letter sized paper.

This is undoubtedly the most challenging design to fold and assemble in this book. The modules will hold together well enough so that the finished model will sit on a tabletop but if you want to be able to pass it around a classroom you will need to glue them together.

These diagrams show you how to make a planar icosidodecahedron using ten modules in each of six colours so that each decagonal plane is coloured independently.

Folding the modules

1

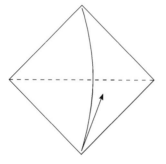

Fold in half downwards, then unfold.

2

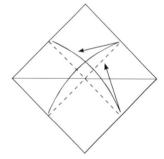

Fold in half edge to edge, then unfold, in both directions.

3

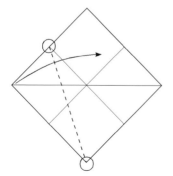

Fold the left corner inwards, making sure the crease begins and ends at the points marked with circles. Do this as accurately as you can.

4

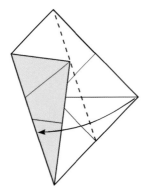

Repeat step 3 on the right corner in the way shown here.

5

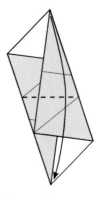

Fold in half downwards.

6

Unfold.

7

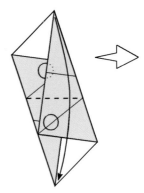

Fold in half downwards again but this time interlock the two front flaps as you do so. The parts of the flaps marked with circles both end up behind the other flap as the fold is made.

8

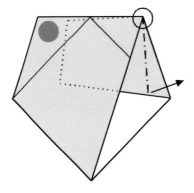

Hold the layers together at the point marked with a dark circle then gently pull out the middle layer so that the internal corner (marked with a dotted line) moves to the position marked with the lower circle in picture 9.

9

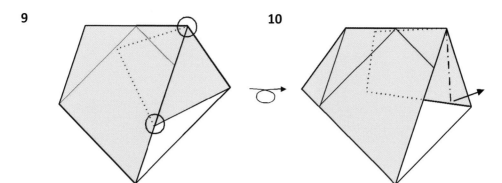

Make sure that the top right corner (marked by the upper circle) has not become damaged. Flatten the folds in their new position then turn over sideways.

10

Repeat fold 8 on this side of the design.

11

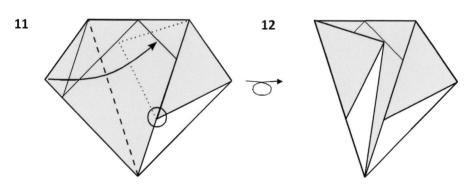

Fold the left point inwards along the line of the right edge of the layers behind it.

12

Turn over sideways.

13

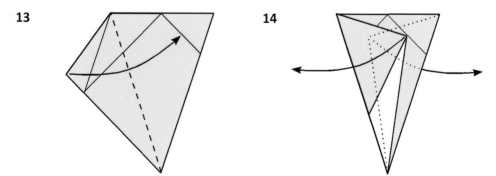

Repeat step 11 on this side of the design.

14

Open out both tabs as shown.

15

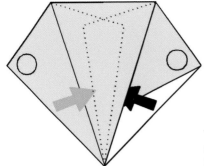

The finished module will look like this. It has two tabs (marked with circles) and two pockets (indicated by arrows). Make all sixty.

Putting the modules together

16

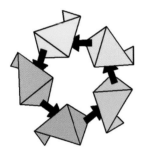

The first five modules go together like this to form a pentagonal ring.

17

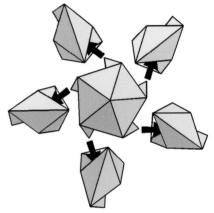

Add ten more modules to surround the pentagonal ring with triangles.

18

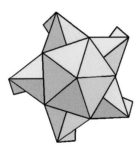

Continue adding modules, keeping to the colour scheme shown in picture 19.

19

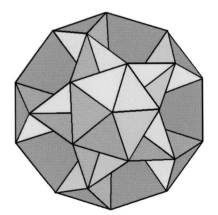

The finished planar icosidodecahedron should look like this.

Making the
Starting Shapes

Making squares

Method 1 - using scissors

1

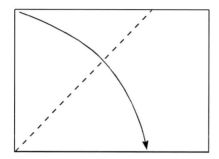

Begin with a sheet of A4 or US letter sized paper. Fold the left hand edge onto the bottom edge. Hold the edges together and crease firmly.

2

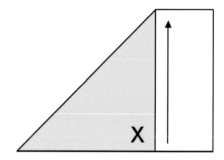

Hold the sheets firmly together and in alignment - especially at point X - and cut carefully along the upright edge working from bottom to top.

3

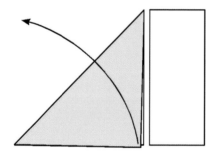

Unfold the square.

4

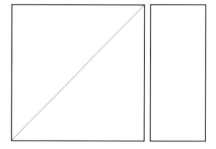

Squares made in this way have a single diagonal crease across them. Use Method 2 if you prefer to avoid ending up with this crease across your squares.

5

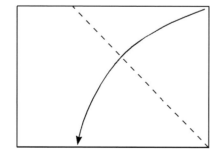

If you are left-handed you will probably find it easiest to make the initial fold in this direction, but the cut should still be made from bottom to top.

Method 2 - using craft knife, metal rule and cutting board

6

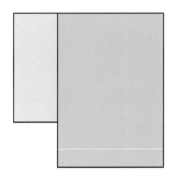

Lay two sheets of paper onto a cutting board and line up the top and right hand edges exactly, like this. Hold both sheets firmly in place.

7

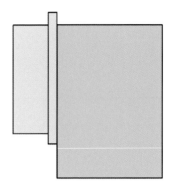

Lay a metal rule exactly along the left hand edge of the top sheet. Hold the rule firmly in place.

8

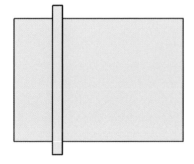

Remove the top sheet. Cut along the right hand edge of the metal rule taking great care that neither the rule nor the paper moves.

9

The result should be a perfect, uncreased square. If your knife is sharp enough you can cut several squares at a time in this way. If you are left-handed, you will probably find it easier to follow these instructions in mirror-image.

Making bronze rectangles

Making the template

1

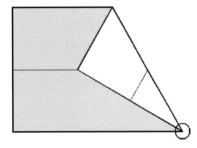

Begin with a sheet of A4 or US letter sized paper. Fold in half downwards, then unfold.

2

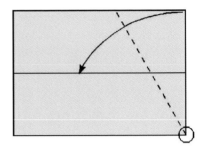

Fold the top right corner onto the horizontal centre crease making sure that the crease begins from the bottom right corner.

3

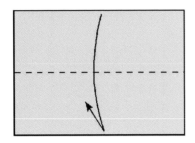

Check that the bottom right corner is sharp and that the left corner of the front layer lies exactly on the horizontal crease. Turn over sideways.

4

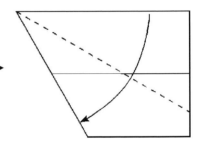

Fold the top edge onto the sloping right hand edge.

5

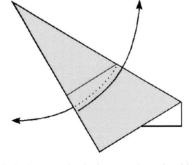

All the layers at both sloping edges should line up exactly. Open out both folds.

6

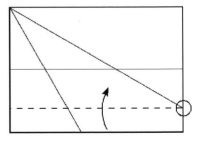

Fold the bottom edge upwards using the point marked with a circle to locate the fold. Once you have done this the template is finished.

Using the template

7

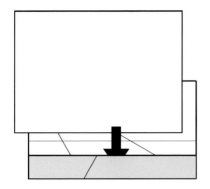

Slide a second sheet of paper inside the pocket in the template as far as it will go.

8

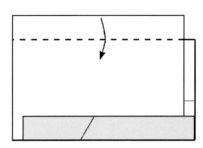

Fold the top edge of the second sheet downwards along the line of the edge of the paper behind it.

9

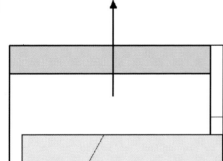

Remove the second sheet from the template.

10

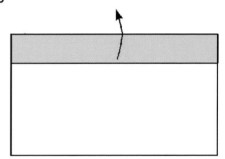

Open out the fold made in step 8.

11

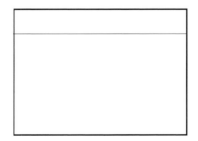

Cut along the horizontal crease.

12

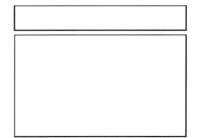

The lower part of the paper is an uncreased bronze rectangle. To make quarter size bronze rectangles fold in half edge to edge, then unfold, in both directions and cut along the new creases you have made.

Making mock platinum rectangles

Making the template

1

Begin with a square of paper made in the way shown on pages 128 and 129 from the same size of rectangle you will be making your mock platinum rectangles from. Fold the bottom edge onto the left edge but only crease the lower third of the fold. Unfold.

2

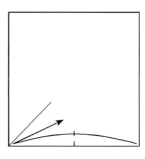

Make a tiny crease to mark the centre of the bottom edge.

3

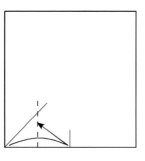

Fold the left edge onto the tiny crease but only crease the lower part of the fold. Make sure the folds made in steps 1 and 3 intersect.

4

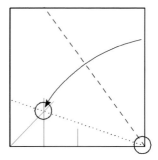

Fold the right edge diagonally inwards so that it touches the point where the creases made in steps 1 and 3 intersect. Make sure the crease starts from the bottom right corner, which becomes sharp.

5

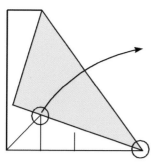

Check that fold 4 has been made completely accurately. Unfold.

6

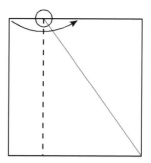

Fold the left edge inwards using the point where the crease made in step 4 intersects the top edge to locate the fold. Once you have done this, the template is finished.

Using the template

7

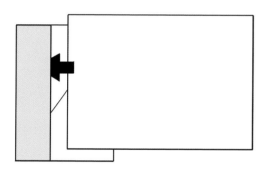

Slide a second sheet of paper inside the pocket in the template as far as it will go.

8

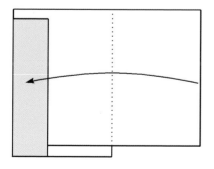

Fold the right edge of the second sheet inwards along the line of the edge of the paper behind it.

9

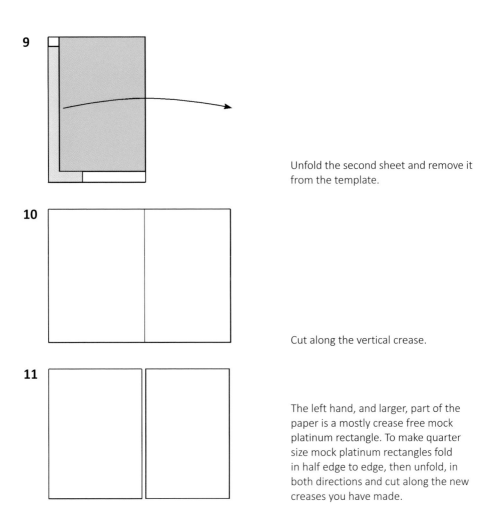

Unfold the second sheet and remove it from the template.

10

Cut along the vertical crease.

11

The left hand, and larger, part of the paper is a mostly crease free mock platinum rectangle. To make quarter size mock platinum rectangles fold in half edge to edge, then unfold, in both directions and cut along the new creases you have made.

Making silver rectangles from US letter sized paper

Making the template

1

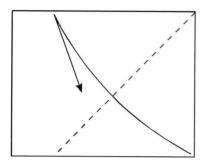

Begin with a sheet of US letter sized paper. Fold the right edge onto the top edge, then unfold.

2

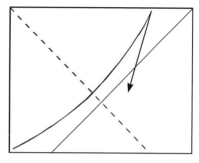

Fold the left edge onto the top edge, then unfold.

3

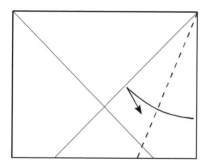

Fold the right edge onto the crease made in step 1, then unfold.

4

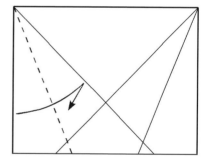

Fold the left edge onto the crease made in step 2, then unfold.

5

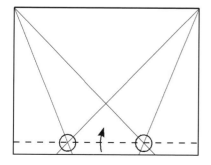

Fold the bottom edge upwards using the points marked with circles to locate the crease. Do this as accurately as possible. Once you have done this the template is finished.

Using the template

6

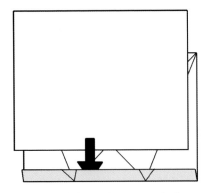

Slide a second sheet of paper inside the pocket in the template as far as it will go.

7

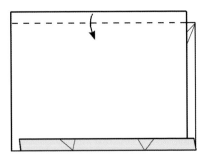

Fold the top edge of the second sheet downwards along the line of the edge of the paper behind it.

8

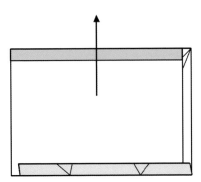

Remove the second sheet from the template.

9

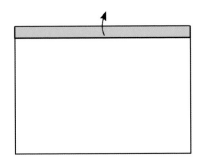

Open out the fold made in step 8.

10

Cut along the horizontal crease.

11

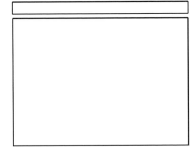

The lower part of the paper is an uncreased silver rectangle. To make half size silver rectangles fold in half short edge to short edge, then unfold, and cut along the new crease you have made. This process can be repeated ad infinitum.

Making silver rectangles from squares

1

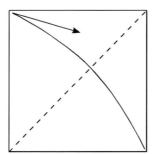

Fold a square in half diagonally, then unfold.

2

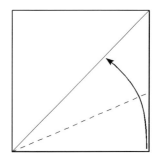

Fold the bottom edge onto the diagonal crease.

3

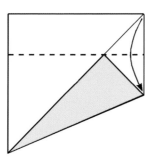

Fold the right hand edge in half downwards.

4

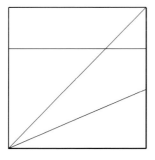

Open out completely.

5

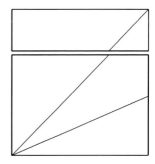

Separate the pieces by cutting along the horizontal crease.

6

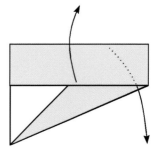

The larger piece is a silver rectangle. By folding the top edge downwards along the existing crease, rather than by cutting it off, you could create a template that could be used in a similar way to the template created in steps 1 to 5 on page 135.

Making golden rectangles

Making the template

1

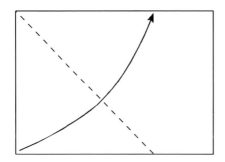

Begin with a sheet of A4 or US letter sized paper. Fold the left edge onto the top edge.

2

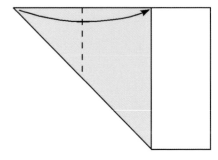

Fold the top left corner onto the top right corner of the front layer.

3

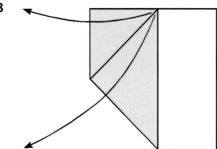

Open out both folds.

4

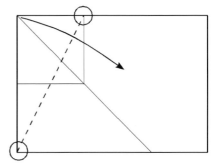

Fold the top left corner inwards making sure the crease forms between the two points marked with circles here.

5

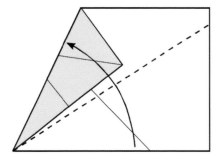

Fold the bottom edge onto the sloping left edge.

6

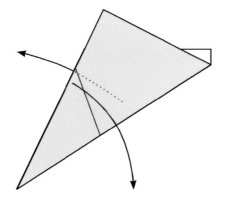

Open out the folds made on steps 4 and 5.

7

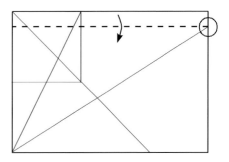

Fold the top edge downwards as shown, using the point marked with a circle to locate the crease.

8

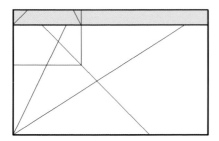

Make sure the crease made in step 7 is exactly parallel to the top edge by lining up the left and right edges. The template is finished. Rotate 90 degrees and align to picture 9.

Using the template

9

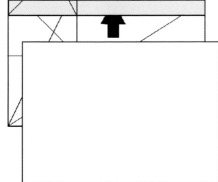

Slide a second sheet of paper inside the pocket in the template as far as it will go.

10

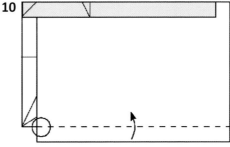

Fold the top edge of the second sheet downwards along the line of the edge of the paper behind it.

11

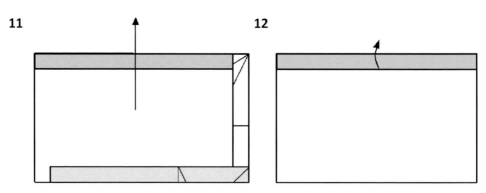

Remove the second sheet from the template.

12

Open out the fold made in step 10.

13

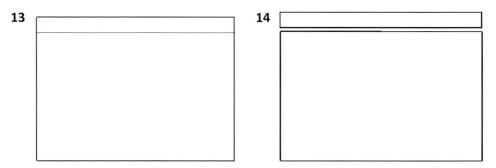

Cut along the vertical crease.

14

The lower hand part of the paper is a crease free golden rectangle. To make quarter size golden rectangles fold in half edge to edge, then unfold, in both directions and cut along the new creases you have made.

Assembly Puzzle
Solutions

Assembly Puzzle Solutions

Four rhombic pyramids in a rhombic tetrahedron

1

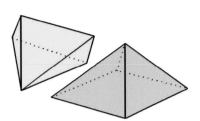

2

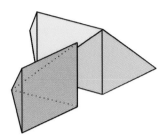

3

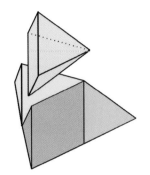

4

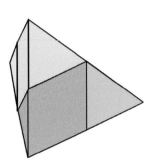

Eight rhombic pyramids in a larger rhombic pyramid

Solution one

1

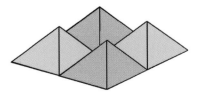

2

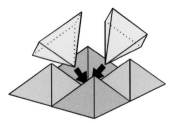

3

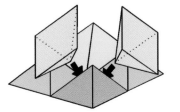

4

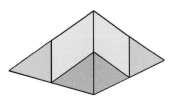

Solution One.

Solutions two and three

1

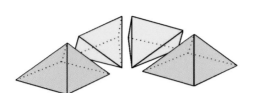

2

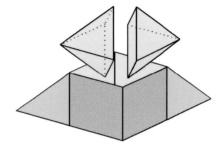

3

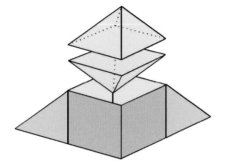

Solution Two.

4

Solution Three.

5

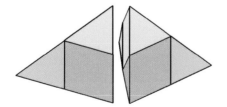

The solution three rhombic pyramid can be split into two rhombic tetrahedra like this.

Acknowledgements

Modular origami design is not an academic discipline and it is sometimes difficult to track the chain of influences, insights and ideas that leads to the discovery of new designs. I have done my best to acknowledge everyone I know has played a part in the development of the designs in this book, but if I have forgotten, over-looked or simply not known about anyone's contribution I apologise and hope you will forgive me.

The first evidence of a modular origami design in Japan is from 1734 and in Western Europe from 1837. However the modular origami idea was not developed further in any substantial way until the mid 1960s when, in Japan, Mitsonobu Sonobe discovered the versatile module that is now generally known to paperfolders as the Sonobe module, and to mathematics teachers as the 'limping seagull', and, in the USA, Robert E Neale found that six waterbomb bases would go together to form a planar octahedron. From that time on various paperfolders in various countries gradually pushed the modular origami idea forward. Many of these advances seem almost blindingly obvious in hindsight, but they were often hard won and revolutionary at the time.

The Sonobe module was first used to make a simple cube but it also proved possible to use it to make any other form that was composed of right-angle isosceles triangles, including some of great complexity. Two of the most important break-throughs came sometime in the mid-1980s when the Japanese paperfolder Tomoko Fuse found that two opposite corners of the Sonobe module could be turned inside out to create pockets and in 1986, when the British paperfolder Nick Robinson discovered that if you applied the crease pattern of this corner-pocket version of the Sonobe module to A4 rather than square paper the result was a module that would make the rhombic dodecahedron and many other related forms.

This clearly showed that the folding method for the corner-pocket version of the Sonobe module would generalise to any other rectangle. I used this insight to produce the equilateral module, which will make the majority of the equilateral deltahedra, from a bronze rectangle, and to produce a regular dodecahedron from the mock platinum rectangle. As far as I know the British paperfolder Jonathan Shapcott was the first to apply the same folding method to a golden rectangle to model the triacontahedron.

In the late 1980's another British paperfolder, David Brill, found that a planar cube could be made from simple modules folded from a silver rectangle and the Japanese paperfolder, Kunihiko Kasahara, realised that this folding method would also generalise and produced a module from a golden rectangle that would make a planar icosahedron. This inspired me to produce planar tetrahedron, planar cuboctahedron and planar icosidodecahedron designs. My friend Ian Harrison independently produced the planar tetrahedron and had the further insight that such tetrahedra could easily be added to the planar cube.

David Mitchell, Arnside, Cumbria